"A beautifully written and expertly re[illegible] most fascinating Catholic artists of our time. Deanna Witkowski, a musician herself, brings to life a whole era in this engrossing new book about art, music, love, perseverance, and faith."

—James Martin, SJ, author of *Learning to Pray* and *In All Seasons, For All Reasons*

"When Mary Lou brought jazz to the Mass, she was inviting us to universal love and the joy of the resurrection. May we all become, like the great Saint Mary Lou Williams, people of universal love."

—Rev. John Dear, author of *Living Peace*, *The Questions of Jesus*, *The Beatitudes of Peace*, and *Lazarus Come Forth* and director of www.beatitudescenter.org

"I had the good fortune of meeting Mary Lou Williams one summer day in the seventies when she came to visit her friend, Dorothy Day, at the Catholic Worker Farm in Tivoli, New York. I've been collecting Williams's recordings ever since. Now there is also Deanna Witkowski's biography. Its author is the pianist who has done so much to introduce a new generation to one of the musical geniuses of the last century."

—Jim Forest, author of *Writing Straight with Crooked Lines: A Memoir*

"In this brief biography, Deanna Witkowski retrieves for Catholics, African American Catholics in particular, the life of jazz virtuoso Mary Lou Williams. Witkowski offers readers a glimpse into the inner life of a 'musical contemplative,' who was one of the great jazz pianists, arrangers, and composers of the 20th century. Although befriended, encouraged, and counseled by several priests and women religious, Mary Lou Williams remains unknown among most African American Catholics. This contribution to the People of God series provides an opportunity for us to discover and appreciate the musical talent and spiritual commitment of one of our own."

—Dr. M. Shawn Copeland, Professor Emerita, Department of Theology, Boston College

"This is a long-overdue study of an important American artist and unconscionably neglected figure in our particular communion of saints. I am an unabashed fan of Mary Lou Williams, this book, and its author. Deanna Witkowski—a jazz pianist, musicologist, and convert to the Catholic faith—is uniquely qualified for her role in Mary Lou's revival. Read these pages, and you'll grow immeasurably richer in history, in music, and in soul."

—Mike Aquilina, EWTN host, author of many books, songwriter, executive vice-president of the St. Paul Center for Biblical Theology

"Deanna Witkowski's *Mary Lou Williams: Music for the Soul* is a thrilling account of the extraordinary life of a brilliantly successful African American jazz artist who became a devout Catholic—and it is so much more besides. The reader who accompanies Mary Lou on her journey bears witness to the historical circumstances that shaped her era: the evolution of jazz music in America, the challenges African American musicians faced as they tried to practice their art, the sexism of the jazz world, the difficult and often tragic lives of professional musicians, and the powerful appeal of the Catholic Church to artists in search of meaning in life, stability, and a spiritual home. Witkowski, as a jazz artist herself who converted to Catholicism, is the ideal person to write this biography of Mary Lou, a figure from the great pantheon of jazz musicians in whom she 'unexpectedly found a soul companion and lifelong mentor.' Her extensive musical knowledge makes her the perfect guide to Williams's work, and her identity as a fellow Catholic enables her to empathize with Mary Lou's spiritual journey. A meticulously researched and well-told tale, *Mary Lou Williams* is rife with cliffhangers, foreshadowing, tragic losses, psychic and religious visions, and unexpected intrusions of grace. It is also, to this reader's delight, a labor of love."

—Angela Alaimo O'Donnell, author of *Flannery O'Connor: Fiction Fired by Faith*

"I've known Deanna Witkowski as a friend and jazz pianist for more than two decades. I've experienced her compassion, her artistry, her gift for translating the sacred into intricate and gorgeous melodies. I've known her as a musician, but now I'm pleased to also know her as an author. I can think of few people better equipped to bring the story and music of Mary Lou Williams to life. Deanna shines brilliant light on Williams's humanity, faith, and immense influence on jazz music. But she also builds a strong case for why Williams was one of our most important modern composers of sacred works. I suspect the music of Mary Lou Williams will be added to many new playlists as a result of this excellent book."

—Edward Gilbreath, author of *Reconciliation Blues* and *Birmingham Revolution*

"Witkowski's book presents Mary Lou Williams as both human and saint. Williams's compassion for the human dilemma and her advocacy for jazz both as musical artform and as the prescription for conveying the love of God to all people is laid bare before the reader. One cannot help but come away from this excursion into the life of Williams with the whole point of the Gospel: love of neighbor. And jazz is the cure. What perhaps is equally as palpable is the role of many in the Catholic Church as patron of the arts. The fact that Mary Lou Williams found spiritual solace in the Catholic faith is not lost on this reader, especially at a time when there is much racial strife in the country and African American Catholics may wonder, 'Where is the Church?' Witkowski's sharing of Williams's journey reminds us of the potential of a home for Black Catholics."

—M. Roger Holland, II, Director of The Spirituals Project, University of Denver

People of God

Remarkable Lives, Heroes of Faith

People of God is a series of inspiring biographies for the general reader. Each volume offers a compelling and honest narrative of the life of an important twentieth- or twenty-first-century Catholic. Some living and some now deceased, each of these women and men has known challenges and weaknesses familiar to most of us but responded to them in ways that call us to our own forms of heroism. Each offers a credible and concrete witness of faith, hope, and love to people of our own day.

John XXIII by Massimo Faggioli
Oscar Romero by Kevin Clarke
Thomas Merton by Michael W. Higgins
Francis by Michael Collins
Flannery O'Connor by Angela O'Donnell
Martin Sheen by Rose Pacatte
Dorothy Day by Patrick Jordan
Luis Antonio Tagle by Cindy Wooden
Joseph Bernardin by Steven P. Millies
Corita Kent by Rose Pacatte
Daniel Rudd by Gary B. Agee
Helen Prejean by Joyce Duriga
Paul VI by Michael Collins
Thea Bowman by Maurice J. Nutt
Shahbaz Bhatti by John L. Allen Jr.
Rutilio Grande by Rhina Guidos
Elizabeth Johnson by Heidi Schlumpf
Augustus Tolton by Joyce Duriga
Paul Farmer by Jennie Weiss Block
Rosemary Nyirumbe by María Ruiz Scaperlanda
James Martin, SJ, by Jon M. Sweeney
Theodore Hesburgh, CSC, by Edward P. Hahnenberg
Nicholas Black Elk, by Jon M. Sweeney

More titles to follow . . .

Mary Lou Williams

Music for the Soul

Deanna Witkowski

LITURGICAL PRESS
Collegeville, Minnesota
www.litpress.org

Cover design by Red+Company. Cover illustration by Philip Bannister.

1 2 3 4 5 6 7 8 9

Library of Congress Control Number: 2021933058

ISBN 978-0-8146-6401-8 978-0-8146-6425-4 (e-book)

Standing apart from a crowd that she is more likely to lead than to follow, Mary Lou Williams can rely on history to accord her a proper place.

—Phyl Garland, "The Lady Lives Jazz," *Ebony* (October 1979)

Contents

Acknowledgments

After having spent more than twenty years performing the music of Mary Lou Williams and researching her life and work, my own life is yielding unexpected, and yet inevitable, gifts. The book you hold in your hands is one of them. My heartfelt thanks go to Andy Edwards and Barry Hudock, who recognized that Williams's story belongs in the People of God series as well as the fact that my perspective as a musician, scholar, and adult convert to Catholicism uniquely qualified me as the person to write this volume.

The largest of my book-related gifts is a city: Williams's welcoming hometown of Pittsburgh. After having spent twenty-three years as a Manhattan apartment dweller, I relocated to Pittsburgh in the fall of 2020. My love affair with the place I call "the city where jazz is love" began with a solo concert I was booked to perform at the Hillman Center at Shadyside Academy in December of 2018, for which I thank Christa Burneff. Knowing that Williams had grown up in Pittsburgh, I decided to arrive nine days early to familiarize myself with the city. At the time, I had one friend here, Bryan Perry, who, along with his beautiful family, hosted me in their Highland Park home. In the course of my stay, I met many musicians and historians of the Pittsburgh jazz scene, gave a keynote performance-lecture on Williams at the University of Pittsburgh where I met some of Williams's relatives, and was featured on the local jazz radio station, WZUM. Thank you to Grace Aquilina and Scott Hanley for these opportunities. I was embraced so wholeheartedly by everyone I encountered that by the time I played my Hillman Center concert on my final night in town, I seriously began to consider what it might be like to live here.

Mary Lou Williams kept bringing me back to Pittsburgh. The following spring, I received an invitation to perform several Williams compositions with the Pittsburgh Symphony Orchestra on a recommendation from producer and guitarist Marty Ashby. On returning again in the fall of 2019 to continue my research and delve deeper into the Pittsburgh jazz scene for seven weeks, Marty met with me to ask how my book was progressing. When I mentioned my desire to record a full album of Williams's compositions—especially as the purpose of this book is to lead the reader to Williams's music—Marty replied, "Well, let's make that happen." After a delay of nine months due to the coronavirus pandemic, in January of 2021, I recorded at Manchester Craftsmen's Guild in Pittsburgh with both local musicians and my regular trio mates, who traveled from New York City and Austin, Texas, to make the sessions. All of these musicians—Daniel Foose, Scott Latzky, Clay Jenkins, Dwayne Dolphin, and Roger Humphries—have encouraged me in ways that have expanded my heart and given me joy. Thanks to Marty's commitment to extending the Pittsburgh jazz legacy, these three days in the studio are documented on my all-Williams recording, *Force of Nature*.

I remain grateful for the entire Pittsburgh jazz community, where fans of the music ply me with questions about Williams and enthusiastically listen to me perform on their bandstands. I am particularly thankful to guitarist John Shannon, who has made me feel at home at Con Alma, the new jazz club that continues the rich legacy of Pittsburgh jazz history, and to drummer Thomas Wendt, who proofread my book chapters with the eye of a jazz historian.

Non-Pittsburghers I must thank include Vincent Pelote, Tad Hershorn, and Elizabeth Surles at the Institute of Jazz Studies at Rutgers University in Newark, New Jersey, where I paid multiple visits to Williams's archives. Thanks also to Williams's late manager, Fr. Peter O'Brien, SJ, who paid me a high compliment when he enthused that I "played the hell out of Mary Lou's 'Gloria'" at a 2013 performance of *Mary Lou's Mass*. Thanks also to Linda Dahl and Tammy Kernodle for their earlier, much-needed biographies of Williams and for their collegiality.

My deep thanks to Don Ottenhoff and the Collegeville Institute for Ecumenical and Cultural Research for hosting me at two invaluable residences: first as a short-term scholar, when I spent a month in quiet, making frequent jaunts uphill to the library at Saint John's University; and several months later in the "Apart, and Yet a Part" writing workshop led by Michael McGregor. Michael's reminder to keep Williams beside me as I wrote was the single greatest help to creating this book, and the encouragement of that group of eleven writers—especially at our 6:30 a.m. Facebook check-ins—carried into my daily work.

I am grateful to my mother, Dale, for providing a place for me to write, sleep, and eat at the start of the coronavirus pandemic when I was unable to return to my former home in New York City. And to Manny, the person who has pushed me the most to keep going, not just with my writing but with every aspect of my life: thank you for believing in me.

Remembering the people who have entered my life over the last three years because of Williams's story, I realize that the biggest gift of this project is that it has widened my circle of friends. For this, I am truly thankful.

Introduction

As a new resident of Mary Lou Williams's hometown of Pittsburgh, I see Williams everywhere. The cigarette-stained keys on her well-worn Baldwin upright piano are on display among belongings of other local jazz legends at the Heinz History Center. She gazes at me from the murals of Pittsburgh icons that appear on downtown buildings and along the East Busway. Minutes after boarding a bus from Saint Benedict the Moor parish in the historic Hill District, I gasp on seeing Williams's image on the side of an old theater as I whiz by. I later find out that the building was the New Granada Theatre (formerly the Pythian Temple and the Savoy Ballroom), a major jazz venue where Ella Fitzgerald, Duke Ellington, and Louis Armstrong performed.

Williams keeps leading me deeper and deeper into the musical legacy of this welcoming city. Less than a year prior to moving here, while renting a room for seven weeks, I often mentioned Williams in conversation. Almost invariably, whether I was speaking with a lifelong Pittsburgh resident, a professional jazz musician, or a college music student, I heard variations on the same refrain: "Wow! Williams was a great pianist, right? And didn't she compose a lot of important jazz tunes? I mean, I don't know any of her pieces. What did she write? Wasn't she a mentor for [pianist] Thelonious Monk?"

These responses reminded me that, to this day, most jazz musicians—let alone historians or Pittsburgh residents rightfully proud of their city's rich jazz legacy—know Williams's name and almost none of her music. Her compositions are not played in piano trios (piano, bass, and drums), one of the standard instrumentations in jazz. And while some of her big band music is available and is starting to receive more programming, it's not yet in the regular repertoire of collegiate or professional jazz orchestras. In the "great man" narrative all too common in jazz history today, Williams is often reduced to a role as an early big band arranger and a mentor to bebop musicians whose names and compositions are front and center in the pantheon of jazz greats, such as Monk, saxophonist Charlie "Bird" Parker, and trumpeter John Birks "Dizzy" Gillespie. Williams's work—her musical output—is understudied and underperformed.

Williams's spiritual journey is also commonly reduced to a one-dimensional story emphasizing how her mid-life conversion to Catholicism made her somewhat of a religious fanatic. Rather than honoring the months of rigorous religious education and decision-making that a person wishing to enter the Catholic faith undertakes prior to baptism, Williams's choice to embrace Catholicism gets glossed over as a retreat from her arduous life as a performer in which "she trusted everybody and was treated so bad."[1] Yet as her friend Dorothy Day knew all too well, Christianity is not simply an interior, personal faith. It requires seeing God in all things—in all people—and demands that we care for the poor in our midst. Williams cared for the poor and, like Day, chose voluntary poverty in order to rehabilitate the sick in her community, especially jazz musicians. She performed these works of mercy even prior to her religious conversion. A 1950 album cover of a recording by pianist Bud Powell shows Williams—partially hidden—and Powell at an upright piano, perhaps at Mary's piano in her Harlem apartment. Mary was a behind-the-scenes, one-woman support system for Powell, not only coaching him musically and recommending him for gigs but calming him when his mental exhaustion turned into explosive episodes, which led to several stays in mental institutions.

Williams's charitable work via her two Manhattan thrift shops and her founding of the Bel Canto Foundation, a charitable nonprofit organization dedicated to rehabilitating jazz musicians who suffered from drug addiction, is well documented. Less discussed is her ministry of letter-writing conducted over decades with fans from all walks of life, including priests and nuns. Williams cultivated nascent friendships by writing to religious sisters who she met during her many spiritual retreats. In the 1960s, her frequent letters to Fr. Michael Williams, the new director of the Catholic Youth Organization in Pittsburgh, facilitated the production of the first Pittsburgh Jazz Festival, a historic piano workshop including Williams, Edward Kennedy "Duke" Ellington, and Willie "the Lion" Smith, and a teaching position at Seton High School where she wrote her first jazz Mass.

Williams found sustenance for her daily work in letters she received from men and women religious as well as from listeners who found healing in her music and her words of encouragement. Her kindheartedness extended to notes she wrote on the backs of torn envelopes from fans who shared how their lives had been transformed after they heeded her admonitions to go back to church or after she spoke with them following a performance. Her scribbled writing often simply said, "Send record [her recordings]." And send she did. Williams gave away everything she had—her scant physical possessions, her apartment, her music, her time—to save the world.

As Dorothy Day said, quoting Dostoevsky, "Beauty will save the world." Williams showed that the discipline, freedom, and beauty inherent in being a jazz musician and a person of faith has the power to heal the troubled soul.

* * *

A further word about my own connection to Williams. As a professional jazz pianist, composer, and liturgical musician, I was introduced to Williams in 1999, when pianist and educator Dr. Billy Taylor invited me to perform at the Kennedy Center's Mary Lou Williams Women in Jazz Festival. On accepting, I realized that I knew almost nothing about the festival's namesake. Like the majority of jazz musicians, I only knew that Williams had been a lauded pianist-composer who had mentored other jazz stars whose music I *did* know. I asked myself why I had never heard any of this woman's music.

My eagerness to learn more about Williams came at an opportune time: *Morning Glory*, a new Williams biography by Linda Dahl, had just been published. Trumpeter Dave Douglas had recently released a Williams tribute album, *Soul on Soul*, so I emailed him asking for a list of essential Williams recordings. I started listening to Mary's music—and, since then, have never stopped.

From Dahl's biography, I learned that Williams was a liturgical jazz pioneer who had composed three Mass settings. I was astonished. Just two years earlier, I had relocated from Chicago to New York to serve as a full-time music director at All Angels' Episcopal Church. I had recently composed my second jazz Mass for the congregation and began presenting my music in churches outside of New York. I realized that I shared a goal with Williams, whether composing for a specific congregation or playing in a jazz club: to make jazz—or, more broadly, all of my original work—*accessible* to all. Like Williams, I believe that jazz should be played everywhere: in the club, at the community center, on the sidewalk, in church. In Williams, I had unexpectedly found a soul companion and lifelong mentor.

Over the intervening years, Mary (whom, from this point on, I will call by her first name) has become more and more a part of my life. As an adult convert to Catholicism who converted through the influence of the Jesuits—even attending a lay spirituality program at the same New York parish where Mary presented "Saint Martin de Porres," her first major liturgical work, in the early 1960s—I began to realize that I was literally walking in Mary's footsteps. As a musician who presents jazz in churches of all different denominations, I often picture Mary seated at the piano in St. Patrick's Cathedral on Fifth Avenue, playing her joyous *Mary Lou's Mass* with her trio in front of 3,000 people as five priests process to the altar. Mary gives me courage. Sometimes I speak with her before I play, knowing that in a very real sense, she has been here before me. Once I began spending extended time in her hometown of Pittsburgh, I came to realize that the warmth I felt in the welcoming, soulful people in the city where she grew up was the same warmth I've experienced in all of Mary's playing. Now I, too, call Pittsburgh home. Each time I step onto the stage to play just mere feet from the Charles "Teenie" Harris photo of her that hangs proudly at the Pittsburgh jazz club Con Alma, I send a quick prayer to Mary, thanking her for being with me, and then I start pressing down the keys, letting the sound, the space, and everything it has taken to get me to this moment, all come out. I hope that a fraction of what I feel when I play is expressed in these pages and that Mary's story will bring you to what, for her, was the most important thing: her music.

CHAPTER ONE

Changing the Scene (1910–26)

> Looking back, I see that my music acted as a shield, preventing me from being aware of many of the prejudices that must have existed. I was completely wrapped up in my music. Little else mattered to me.
>
> —Mary Lou Williams, quoted in Linda Dahl, *Morning Glory: A Biography of Mary Lou Williams*

In many interviews over the last twenty years of her life, Mary Lou Williams gave a particular narrative of her life story, rarely going off script. Starting with her mother's recognition of her young daughter's extraordinary musical gift, her moniker at the age of six as "the little piano girl of East Liberty," and her gigs on the road beginning at the age of twelve, Mary's life confirmed that she would always be a musician. Music for Mary was both a refuge and a vehicle for spreading love in communities separated by race and fear, even among neighbors who welcomed her family to Pittsburgh by throwing bricks through their windows. She tended to her gift and trusted it as her lifelong companion, more than any human relationship. She also believed in the bonds of family and community, and gave away all that she could to help her relatives and musicians in need. Mary's music and her unyielding belief in its power to heal gave her the strength, stubbornness, and stamina to forge a life as a pioneering jazz musician in a field where she saw few others who looked like her. Her knowledge that she was different began with a sign at her birth.

* * *

On May 8, 1910, Mary Elfrieda Scruggs was born as the second of eight children to Virginia Riser in the Edgewood neighborhood of Atlanta, Georgia. The midwife who delivered Mary told her mother that her daughter had been born with a "veil," a thin membrane of placenta, over her eyes. In African American culture, children born with such a veil were believed to have the gift of second sight—an ability to see visions that were not apparent to others. In his 1903 book *The Souls of Black Folk*, W. E. B. Du Bois describes the "veil" as a symbol of double consciousness for African Americans, who knew that their true identities were not recognized by white society. As a child who was viewed as "different" because of her frequent visions and her musical ability, and throughout her life as an African American and as a woman, Mary had to have a strong sense of self in order to break through many constant but unseen barriers.

Mary's extraordinary perception extended to her sense of hearing. Her mother, Virginia, was a live-in domestic who was allowed to visit her family only twice per month. On the weekends when she was at home, she danced and played a reed organ in a local Baptist church on Sundays. Holding three-year-old Mary on her lap as she practiced, Virginia was astonished one day when Mary reached up to the keys and played back exactly what she had just heard her mother play. Mary recalled, "It must have really shaken my mother. She actually dropped me and ran out to get the neighbors to listen to me."[1] Mary claimed that from this point on, she never left the instrument. As a young girl, Virginia had taken piano lessons, but felt that she had lost her ability to improvise after studying with a teacher. Fearing that Mary might suffer the same fate, Virginia would not let a "regular" music teacher near her daughter. In lieu of traditional lessons, Mary soaked up music from traveling performers who frequently visited her home. In later years, Mary's firm belief that jazz could not be taught out of books became a core aspect of her musical philosophy.

In her family's shotgun house, so named because if a gun was "fired through the front door, the shot passed through all the rooms and out into the backyard,"[2] Mary lived with her mother, Virginia; her sister, Mamie, four years her senior; her aunt Anna Mae; her grandparents Anna Jane and Andrew Riser; and her great-grandmother Matilda Parker. Until she was twelve or thirteen, Mary thought that her biological father was Mose Winn, a man Virginia had been married to for a short time just after Mary's birth. It was only through a stinging comment from a relative that Mary learned that she had been born out of wedlock and that her real father was a man named Joseph Scruggs. Although Scruggs was not involved in Mary's life, Willis, his son and Mary's half brother, helped Mary in her early practice sessions on the reed organ by pumping the pedals, as she was too short to reach them herself.

When she was five, Mary's family moved to Pittsburgh, an industrial center of coal and steel production, where her mother hoped to find a better life. Virginia was not alone in choosing the Smoky City as an escape from the poverty of the rural South. Many families, including "northern Blacks" from states such as Maryland and North Carolina, came to Pittsburgh as part of the Great Migration in the early 1900s. Producing 40 percent of the country's steel before the start of World War I, the city had already grown exponentially in the late 1800s when Eastern European immigrants arrived to work in the steel mills. Tension in the highly segregated city existed not only between races but between Blacks who had migrated from different parts of the country. Fortunately, Mary's family had relatives in the North: Virginia's grandparents were already living in the Steel City and two of her aunts were in Philadelphia. Fletcher Burley, Virginia's beau and the man who would soon become Mary's stepfather, made plans to come join the family several months later.

Arriving to the smoke-filled city by train, Mary's family settled in the East Liberty neighborhood, four miles from downtown Pittsburgh. While living between two white families, the family endured acts of prejudice: Mary herself recalled that bricks were thrown through their windows. Undaunted by fear, Mary became a goodwill ambassador by playing piano in neighbors' homes. Her mother was unaware of her daughter's visits until neighbors began appearing at the family's house to ask what had happened to "the little piano girl" after Mary broke her arm while playing with friends. Mary recalled, "Not knowing it, I think my little visits changed the entire scene, and love began to flow."[3]

After Fletcher Burley joined Mary's family in Pittsburgh in 1916, he and Virginia were married. The first of six Burley children, their son Howard was born three years later when Mary was nine. Fletcher encouraged Mary's music making, buying her a player piano and often requesting that she play two of his favorite styles of music, blues and boogie-woogie.

By slowing down the piano rolls, Mary learned classical pieces as well as solos by ragtime pianist Jelly Roll Morton and James P. Johnson, the originator of stride piano. Mary's talent was soon noticed at Lincoln Elementary School. As in all Pittsburgh public schools in the 1920s, Lincoln had no African American teachers. White teachers taught Mary's classmates, themselves a mix of Irish, Italian, and African American. In third grade, while hiding under her great-grandparents' bed, Mary overheard stories of the atrocities her relatives had endured while growing up as slaves under white owners. Mary was so infuriated that when she arrived at school the following day, she hit one of her teachers with a ruler, saying, "You hate black people and I hate white people."[4] Feeling empathy for Mary, her teacher brought her to the attention of the principal, Miss Mulholland. Learning that Mary was a gifted pianist with perfect pitch, Mulholland soon began taking her to afternoon tea at Carnegie Tech (now Carnegie Mellon University), where she would improvise on popular classical pieces. Back at school, Mary would play a march to get the students to walk up the stairs, occasionally segueing into a boogie-woogie for her classmates to dance. School was also where Mary's love of shoes developed: without enough money to purchase shoes that fit, Mary walked to school barefoot and then slipped into a pair of her mother's oxfords during the day, her heels hanging over the back. After classes she took off the shoes to walk home, again barefoot.

Mary soon found that her music could bring in much-needed income. Her stepfather, Fletcher, would bring her with him to poker games, sneaking Mary in under his large overcoat. On arriving, Mary would sit down at a piano to play while Fletcher placed a dollar in his hat and passed it around, encouraging others to add to the kitty. At the end of the night, he gave all of the money, minus his start-up dollar, to Mary. Fletcher's pride in his stepdaughter gave Mary the confidence to perform in any type of environment. Another early supporter who encouraged Mary's musical growth was her brother-in-law, Hugh Floyd. After Mamie, Mary's sixteen-year-old sister, married Hugh, Mary moved out of her mother's house to live with the couple. An amateur saxophonist, Hugh often took Mary to the Hill District, the center of African American musical and cultural life in Pittsburgh, where Mary heard traveling vaudeville performers as well as local musicians including singer Lois Deppe and pianist Earl "Fatha" Hines. Pianist Jack Howard became one of Mary's major influences, showing her how to play her left hand louder than her right because, as Mary explained, "that's where the beat and the feeling was. It's just like a drum keeping a steady beat."[5] While most of the pianists Mary heard—and saw—were men, there was one female player who stood out. Lovie Austin, a Chicago-based pianist and recording artist, was performing locally at a theater on Frankstown Avenue. On seeing Austin perform in the orchestra pit, Mary was in awe, recalling, "She sat cross-legged at the piano, a cigarette in her mouth, writing music with her right hand while accompanying the show with her swinging left! Impressed, I told myself: 'Mary, you'll do that one day.' "[6] Indeed, Mary accomplished the same ambidextrous feat while touring with Andy Kirk and the Clouds of Joy in the 1930s.

In 1924, Mary started at Westinghouse High School, a school that boasts a storied alumni of jazz musicians including pianists Earl Hines, Billy Strayhorn, and Erroll Garner, but soon left to join a traveling vaudeville show called Hits and Bits. Buzzin' Harris, the group's leader, visited Mary's home to audition her for the piano opening on the recommendations of local musicians. When he arrived, he saw her outside playing hopscotch and initially thought he had been played as the brunt of a joke. His feeling changed when Mary sat down and played a ragtime piece and then quickly picked up the tunes Harris hummed to her to learn by ear. Amazed, he immediately asked Mary's mother for permission to bring Mary on the road. Virginia agreed after arranging for a friend to travel with her daughter as a chaperone, and Mary left school two months early to perform at regional theaters on the TOBA (Theatre Owners' Booking Association) circuit. Featuring all-Black shows performed for all-Black audiences, TOBA venues were known among performers as "Tough on Black Asses" because of their harsh working environments, which often did not even provide working bathrooms for performers. Regardless, the taste of being on the road whet Mary's appetite for the life of a touring musician.

Back in Pittsburgh, Mary played solo engagements for the wealthy Mellon family and performed with local union bands. Traveling musicians brought her to their gigs where they would spend hours "jamming" at various clubs stretching from East Liberty to the Hill District. They often ended up at the Subway, a club on Wylie Avenue that Mary remembered as "a hole in the ground to which the cream of the crop came to enjoy the finest in the way of entertainment. For me it was a paradise."[7] If Mary's mind was always on music, others were looking out for her safety. Roland Mayfield, a wealthy man known as "the Black prince of East Liberty," befriended Mary; he gave her rides in his Cadillac to the venues where she performed and taught her how to drive. Mayfield viewed himself as Mary's protector and was the person she called on many occasions when she was stranded after an out-of-town theater refused to pay the musicians. Mayfield showed up with his Cadillac throughout

Mary's life, even driving her back and forth between Pittsburgh and New York as late as the 1960s.

With her many performance requests, Mary did not stay in school for long. After her first tour, she returned to Westinghouse for the fall semester, but in December, Fletcher became ill and was unable to work. In an effort to support her family, Mary went back on the road with Hits and Bits. Playing in Chicago in the winter of 1925, she met her idol Lovie Austin and trumpeter Louis Armstrong. In Cincinnati, a baritone saxophonist named John Williams joined the band. John recalled his reaction on hearing Mary for the first time: "She hit on the piano and I'd never heard nothing like that in my life. Terrific. She outplayed any piano player I'd ever played with. She played note for note anything that she heard . . . and heavy like a man, not light piano. At fourteen."[8] At nineteen, John was well liked and became the show's musical director. He soon began courting Mary, who, though initially reluctant, eventually gave in to his advances. Mary feared that her mother would force her to stop traveling if she did not have the protection of a man. Indeed, many traveling performers became couples simply to split the cost of living expenses. In later interviews, both Mary and John claimed there was never much love between them. Mary explained bluntly, "My music was always first. I didn't love him."[9]

After a year on the road, Hits and Bits disbanded in Kansas City when work ran out. Under John's leadership, the band's instrumentalists had formed a sextet called the Syncopators. When he heard that the popular dance duo, Seymour James and Jeanette Taylor, were performing at the Pantages Theater and were searching for an instrumental group, John booked an audition. Seymour and Jeanette, as they were known professionally, performed on the all-white

Keith-Orpheum circuit, a step up from TOBA venues. Due to heart issues that left him short of breath, Seymour had decided to shorten the duo's performances and add a short jazz set. After a successful audition, the Syncopators toured with the duo throughout the Midwest before arriving in New York on Easter Sunday of 1926. Since vaudeville acts had summers off, after two months of playing regional theaters, Mary had time to explore the music in Harlem, where she met James P. Johnson and Jelly Roll Morton, the pianists whose solos she had learned from the rolls on her player piano in Pittsburgh.

Stimulated by a summer spent listening to musicians she had idolized for a decade, and with a full ten-month season ahead of her with Seymour and Jeanette, Mary was inspired and happy. But after just three weeks on the road in the fall of 1926, Seymour became too ill to continue the tour, and John and Mary had no choice but to return to Pittsburgh. Although Mary's first extended period on the road had been cut short, she would soon begin a twelve-year stretch in a popular band that would secure her reputation as one of the foremost swing pianist-composers in the country.

CHAPTER TWO

Eleven Men and a Girl (1927–42)

> Where's the girl? We liked her style.
>
> —Jack Kapp, quoted in Andy Kirk, as told to Amy Lee, *Twenty Years on Wheels*

At the age of sixteen, Mary set to work seemingly packing a lifetime of experience into a single year: 1926 was the year she was first recorded in Chicago; the year she played for one of her idols, pianist Thomas "Fats" Waller, in New York; and the year that she married. While briefly living with John's parents in Memphis, Mary and John were married in a civil ceremony on November 10. But over the next decade, both Mary and John had romantic affairs. John initially attempted to cover his dalliances, forbidding Mary to socialize with "band wives" when he did not want her to see him in public with another woman he had promised to marry. Not that Mary had money to spend on going out: John gave her a budget of a dollar a day, and she had no work to supplement her meager allowance. Of her feelings toward John, Mary explained, "I couldn't have cared less about what he was doing. I feared John more than I loved him and had begun to dislike him intensely."[1]

Although they were married, Mary and John's struggles to find sufficient work often kept them apart. In 1928 while the couple was living in Memphis, John relocated to Tulsa to join the Clouds of Joy, a territory band that was making a name for itself playing throughout the Midwest. When Mary eventually joined him several months later, driving the 500-mile trip in her "red bathtub" of a Chevrolet, she arrived without employment. As Mary and John's apartment was located above a funeral home, Mary took a job driving a hearse for the undertaker. But a few months later, immediately after receiving news of her stepfather's death, she returned to Pittsburgh, where she visited with her sister Mamie and performed in the Hill District (and enjoyed a hiatus from her stingy husband). Mary's respite was brief. When the Clouds came through Pittsburgh, John insisted that Mary leave with them to travel to their new headquarters in Kansas City, where the band was scheduled to play at the all-white Pla-Mor Ballroom.

Mary's life was about to change dramatically. After months of frustration, she found "Kaycee," as Kansas City was called, to be a "heavenly city" with "music everywhere in the Negro section of town . . . the town was wide open for drinking, gambling, and pretty much every form of vice. Naturally, work was plentiful for musicians."[2] Under the leadership of political "boss" Tom Pendergast, gambling, liquor, and prostitution were three of the city's best known industries. Neither Prohibition nor the stock market crash of 1929 seemed to have any effect on the city's jumping nightlife. After-hours jam sessions with tenor saxophonist Lester Young, alto saxophonist Charlie Parker, and players from local bands led by Bennie Moten and, later, pianist William "Count" Basie were held at clubs clustered near the intersection of 18th and Vine Streets. It was here where Mary had her first real opportunities to showcase her playing while sitting in at jam sessions or in bands led by her close friend, trombonist Jack Teagarden. Mary became a part of the distinctive Kansas City jazz sound, which was heavily influenced by the blues as well as by the virtuosity and freedom that improvising musicians brought to the bandstand. She developed new compositional ideas by listening to visiting East Coast big bands such as Fletcher Henderson's popular New York band, which performed in a "battle of the bands" with Andy Kirk's band in September of 1929.

Even though Mary was not a member of the Clouds, Kirk frequently met with her, showing her how to notate her ideas for new musical arrangements for the band, something he had done since the ensemble's early days in Tulsa. His guidance helped Mary learn to read music, a skill she had bypassed thus far with her ability to instantly play back what she heard. Kirk began having Mary workshop her new compositions in band rehearsals, where she tried out new ideas and learned on the job. In Mary, Kirk found a key to his band's success: an innovative composer-arranger writing specifically for his group. But while Kirk knew of Mary's pianistic abilities, the piano chair in the Clouds was already covered by Marion "Jack" Jackson.

Soon Mary was heard beyond Kansas City. In the fall of 1929, two Chicago record executives came to town in search of a new band for the Brunswick and Vocalion record labels and invited the Clouds to audition. Label executive Jack Kapp wanted to capitalize on the success of "race records," recordings marketed to African American consumers that had seen huge sales in releases by local bandleader Bennie Moten on the rival Okeh label. When the hour arrived for the Clouds' audition at the Pla-Mor, pianist Marion Jackson was nowhere to be found. After some prodding from John, Kirk called on Mary to fill in. In later years, Kirk reflected, "No one had the wildest idea she'd be a big factor in our landing an excellent two-year recording contract, or, wilder yet, that she would make jazz history."[3]

Winning the recording contract, the Clouds went into local radio station KMBC to record eight pieces, including three of Mary's originals: "Mess-a-Stomp," "Blue Clarinet Stomp," and "Froggy Bottom." Especially on "Mess-a-Stomp," Mary's synthesis of Kansas City swing and her inventive sense of harmony showed a glimmer of how Kirk's band could stand out with Mary in its regular cohort. But after the session, Jackson returned to his role as ensemble pianist, and Mary to her intermittent role as chauffeur, driving the Clouds to their one-nighters throughout the Midwest. The band began to travel farther afield when Kirk agreed to substitute for Fletcher Henderson for six weeks in New York. Mary traveled with the band, often playing her solo compositions between sets at the Savoy Ballroom. But without steady employment, she soon went back to Kansas City alone.

The following spring, Mary received a wire asking that she come to Chicago for the Clouds' Brunswick recording date. Not realizing that Mary was not the band's regular pianist, when the Clouds arrived with Jackson on piano, Kapp had asked, "Where's the girl? We liked her style."[4] Uninterested in recording the band without Mary, Kapp told Kirk to get her to Chicago.

Catching a train to St. Louis and then on to Chicago, Mary was sexually assaulted while traveling. The only passenger in her car, she awoke to a man—the conductor—attempting to rape her. While this was not Mary's sole experience of sexual violence, it was something she left out of her many public writings and interviews, only revealing details in her diary. Of her assault on the train, she wrote, "I screamed and looked around, but it was the conductor. I had to fight like mad. I wasn't fit for anything when I arrived in Chicago that morning, but I went straight to the studio to record."[5]

Five days before Mary recorded anything with the Clouds, she played two solo improvisations that, unbeknownst to her, Kapp recorded. "Night Life" and "Drag 'Em," both recorded on April 24, 1930, show Mary's seemingly unstoppable flow of ideas and her abilities as a complete jazz musician at the age of seventeen. If she had recorded nothing else on this session, her status as a major pianist to watch should have been readily apparent. But this is not all that Mary recorded. Among the six sides that the Clouds made in this spring session, Mary's composition "Mary's Idea" stands out as an example of the mix of relaxed Kansas City swing and intricate East Coast harmonic sensibilities that would soon define Kirk's band as a major swing orchestra of the 1930s. Kapp recognized that Mary was creating a new sound that needed to be heard.

Kapp also unexpectedly provided a christening of the name that Mary would be known by for the rest of her life. Prior to the Brunswick date, she had been known as Mary Louise Winn or Mary Lou Burley. It was Kapp who suggested that Mary use her husband's surname and call herself Mary Lou Williams.

* * *

Even though Mary recorded intermittently with the Clouds throughout 1930, she still was not the group's regular pianist. Off the road, her relationship with John continued to deteriorate. During one of the band's tours when Mary stayed at home, John left her without any money for daily needs. When Mary asked him for a new pair of I. Miller shoes, John "blew his stack, saying I should be happy to get $2 for shoes. He knew I had holes in my shoes and no winter coat, yet refused to give me money." Mary temporarily moved in with Kirk's wife, Mary Kirk, herself a pianist, who fed her and gave her a suit coat to wear. Mary recalled, "After this, he [John] looked ugly to me and I'd sit up all night to keep from being in bed with him."[6]

To fight boredom, Mary started playing cards, something that later became a gambling addiction. But her daily life was about to change. In early 1931, the Clouds played an extended engagement in Philadelphia at the Pearl Theatre with singer Blanche Calloway, the older sister of the swing bandleader Cab Calloway. To match Blanche's flamboyant performance style, Kirk decided to feature two pianists as a novelty with Jackson at the Steinway baby grand and Mary at what she called a "Tom Thumb" upright. Drummer Ben Thigpen played on a platform above the pianists, so that Mary complained of being able to hear only "the thunder of drums overhead."[7] But she was on the gig.

One evening, in a throwback to the band's KMBC radio session, Marion Jackson again was nowhere to be found when the band was scheduled to begin, and Mary graduated to the Steinway. When Jackson eventually arrived in a state unfit to perform, Pearl owner Sam Stiefel fired him, telling Kirk, "You don't need him. Keep her—she's great!"[8] Jackson was given two weeks' pay and a ticket home, and Mary became the band's permanent pianist.

For the next five years Mary performed with the Clouds throughout the Southwest and Midwest as well as in their home base of Kansas City. While "Kaycee" may not have felt the full effects of the Depression, the band experienced what Mary termed their "starvation days" in other parts of the country. Live entertainment was being replaced by the rise of radio. Ballrooms that still remained could rarely afford weekly or monthly engagements, forcing Kirk to string together a series of one-nighters to book a tour. He often was not paid at the end of the night. Mary joked, "When Kirk came backstage after a job with his head down, we'd know he hadn't been paid. Instead of gettin' angry or quittin' or running off, we'd just laugh."[9] But these unpaid dates often left the band stranded with no way to get home.

While money was scarce on the road, Mary continued to feel at ease in Kansas City and loved the camaraderie of the Clouds. After finishing their nightly gig at midnight, Mary and many of the band members would play at the Subway, "Piney" Brown's club on 12th Street, where musicians were always fed and cared for. Mary's friendships with several instrumentalists morphed into romantic relationships—indeed, Mary often said that she "fell in love with the sound of a horn." Both John and Mary were open with each other about their affairs. Mary's deepest and longest lasting relationship was with tenor saxophonist Ben Webster, who was a member of the Clouds in 1933 and 1934. The two were fixtures in after-hours jam sessions. One night tenor saxophonist Coleman Hawkins came through town and sat in at the Subway. Mary had gone to bed but woke up at 4 a.m. "to hear someone pecking on my screen. I opened the window on Ben Webster. He was saying, 'Get up, pussycat, we're jammin' and all the pianists are tired out now. Hawkins has got his shirt off and is still blowing. You got to come down.' " Apparently, Hawkins had not been aware of the stamina of local tenor saxophonists Webster, Lester Young, and Herschel Evans, all of whom had lined up in the club to play in a "cutting contest." Mary proudly described the scene: "He [Hawkins] kept trying to blow something to beat Ben and Herschel and Lester. When at last he gave up, he got straight in his car and drove to St. Louis. I heard he'd just bought a new Cadillac and that he burnt it out trying to make the [next] job on time."[10]

Mary's romantic entanglements outside of her marriage to John, who was still in the band, were beginning to affect her work. She had dated several men in the Clouds including saxophonists Webster and Don Byas, both of whom were heavy drinkers who became physically abusive. When Byas hit Mary in public on a job, Kirk fired him and advised Mary to leave the men alone. After Webster left to join Fletcher Henderson's band in 1934, Mary's sadness at the loss of her companion left her unable to eat and she lost twenty-five pounds.

No matter the status of her personal relationships, Mary's musical star was about to rise. A turning point for Kirk's band came in Oklahoma City in 1934 at the whites-only Blossom Heath ballroom. The venue had a regular radio broadcast that reached several states. Since radio did not divulge skin color, promoters, not knowing that the members of the Clouds were Black, requested that the band perform in their venues. Managers began to clamor for Kirk's attention, and soon Kirk accepted an offer to work with booking agent Joe Glaser. Glaser secured a second recording date with Jack Kapp—the band's first since their debut five years earlier—in March of 1936. These sessions would put Mary on the map as a star arranger and pianist.

The new recordings featured Mary's "Walkin' and Swingin'," now a standard in big band repertoire, and a new version of "Froggy Bottom" that became a jukebox hit. Mary's new work would not have received much publicity had it not been for a new hit by other songwriters that was almost scrapped from the date. Kirk wanted to record "Until the Real Thing Comes Along," a "sweet" vocal ballad featuring crooner Pha Terrell. But Kapp's initial response on hearing the tune was, "Andy, what's the matter with you? . . . Why do you want to do what the white boys are doing?"[11] Kapp was still of the opinion that the Clouds' recordings should be marketed strictly to all-Black audiences. Kirk, on the other hand, wanted his recordings to reflect the range of styles—both "hot" sounding swing numbers and "sweet" sounding ballads—that the Clouds were already performing live for both Black and white audiences. Kapp was adamant that Kirk record "Christopher Columbus," a popular swing tune that he predicted would become a hit in the race records market. The two men finally reached a compromise and both songs appeared on the 1936 recordings, with "Until the Real Thing Comes Along" selling 100,000 copies and charting on the brand-new *Billboard* magazine hit parade.

This wider exposure led to new offers for Mary. In 1937, producer John Hammond suggested that Benny Goodman contract Mary to write for him. Mary composed two pieces for the popular clarinetist's swing orchestra: "Camel Hop," the theme song for Goodman's Camel cigarettes–sponsored radio show; and "Roll 'Em," a boogie-woogie number that derived its title from Ben Webster's calling out to boogie-woogie pianist Pete Johnson to "roll 'em, Pete, make 'em jump" at the Sunset Club in Kansas City.[12] Goodman soon asked Mary to arrange exclusively for his band and later offered her the piano chair in his trio, but Mary turned him down, preferring to stay with Kirk. She was gaining recognition as a top-notch arranger and composed steadily for bandleaders including Duke Ellington. Mary estimated that she "was writing for some half-dozen bands each week. As we were making perhaps 500 miles per night, I used to write in the car by flashlight between engagements. . . . I wrote many arrangements while playing with the band on the stand, playing with my left hand and writing with my right."[13] Mary was emulating her early idol Lovie Austin, whom she had seen as a child in Pittsburgh.

Mary had become a new star in the African American community. On one occasion, word got out that she would be arriving at Manhattan's Grand Central Station. David Kane, a reporter from the historic Black newspaper the *Pittsburgh Courier*, spied Mary "hiding" behind a tall column in the massive terminal and deprecatingly described her as "trembling with fear" at seeing press agents gathered to speak with her. Managing to hail the same taxi as Mary while concealing his identity, Kane spoke with her on her ride uptown to 125th Street. Kane wrote that Mary was "just a shy little girl . . . a sweet lovable character whom anyone would love." Yet he also recognized that she had "a deep musical soul" and declared that "Mary Lou Williams stands alone in the world of 'Swing' in the same manner as Paderewski or Horowitz stand out in the world as two of the foremost concert pianists."[14]

A year later Kane again profiled Mary after the release of another Kirk hit, "Little Joe from Chicago," with music and lyrics by Mary and trombonist Henry Wells. Selling 21,000 copies within the first ten days of its release, the boogie-woogie tune featured lyrics that profiled Joe Glaser as a wealthy man who "wears a big blue diamond ring" and "never learned a grammar rule/but how he handles money, makes you know/he's nobody's fool."[15] While the lyric may have been tongue in cheek, it expressed the beginning of Mary's discontent with the Kirk organization. Having turned down multiple offers to join other bands, Mary felt betrayed when her name was replaced on band marquees by vocalist June Richmond and guitarist Floyd Smith. Both Mary and Pha Terrell had repeatedly asked for raises for the entire band without success, and Mary was not paid any royalties for her original compositions. But even more of an issue was Mary's sense that the camaraderie between band members was disappearing. In an article from the mid-1950s, she wrote, "Towards the end . . . there was no more brotherly love. I had lost so much through thefts that for a solid year I had to sleep with everything I owned. When someone broke in my trunk and took earrings, Indian-head pennies and silver dollars which I cherished, I decided to leave."[16]

Mary had split up with John in late 1938, and John had already left the Clouds to join saxophonist Coleman Hawkins's big band. Before their divorce was finalized in early 1942, Mary began seeing trumpeter Harold "Shorty" Baker. Beyond any personal disappointments, Mary had begun to recognize that her musical talent required a larger outlet than the Clouds, where she was now expected to perform her solos exactly the same way as they were recorded. As an improviser who loved to experiment, Mary had more freedom in the several recordings where she was the leader, especially in her January 1940 septet album, *Six Men and a Girl*. She now wanted more opportunities where she could make her own decisions regarding how to express herself as a pianist and composer.

Kirk had recognized from her very first recordings that Mary's "ideas were new all the time"[17] and must have not been too surprised when she left the Clouds in the winter of 1942. While Mary described her exit as happening at a road stop, where she dramatically dragged her suitcase off the tour bus and headed to Pittsburgh, Kirk recalled a more quiet departure during a Washington, DC, performance. His version of events revealed that on top of her musical and personal frustrations, Mary had to do battle with shoddy instruments: "At some point . . . Mary Lou got up from the piano and walked out. I didn't even know she'd left. We sometimes had to play without the piano, as when one was so out of tune she would give up on it rather than try to transpose all night. . . . I can hear her now, playing a chord or two on each piano as we came on a job, and saying, 'I guess I'll have to transpose all night.' "[18] Regardless of which account is accurate, Mary walked away from the band that had been her musical family for twelve years, choosing to find her own path as a soloist and bandleader in her own right.

CHAPTER THREE

Waltz Boogie (1942–52)

It's difficult for a creative artist to live; there are all kinds of obstacles. But as long as you keep your music broad in its scope, fresh in its ideas and experimental, you'll make it.

—Mary Lou Williams, quoted in Barry Ulanov, "Mary Lou Williams," *Metronome* (July 1949)

Prior to moving to Manhattan in the spring of 1942, Mary visited her sister Mamie in Pittsburgh. Harold Baker was still on the road, but after a one-nighter in the Steel City with the Clouds, he never got back on the band bus, choosing to stay behind with Mary. Kirk filed complaints against the couple with Local 802, the New York musicians' union, for breach of contract. Mary risked facing a lawsuit if she did not return to Kirk's band, but she successfully negotiated with the union and did not return to the Clouds.

Mary considered the idea of abandoning public performance completely, but a persistent young drummer named Art Blakey changed her mind. Knocking at Mamie's front door every day for two months, Blakey repeatedly asked Mary to form a group with him. She finally gave in and formed a sextet featuring Blakey, Baker, and tenor saxophonist Orlando Wright. Needing a place to perform, Mary contacted producer John Hammond, who had wanted to work with Mary for years. In 1938, he had set up a date for her to record with vocalist Billie Holiday, but Mary had been temporarily hospitalized for what she called "female troubles" and could not make the session. Now Hammond booked Mary's new group into Mason's Farm, a popular Cleveland nightclub, for a three-month run beginning in August of 1942. The original group was short-lived: when Duke Ellington came through Cleveland, he hired Baker to join his orchestra. After replacing Baker with Pittsburgher Marion "Boonie" Hazel, Mary traveled with her sextet to New York to perform for four weeks at Kelly's Stable, a jazz club on "the Street," as 52nd Street between Fifth and Seventh Avenues was known. But Mary was unhappy with Hazel's playing and quit the engagement, deciding instead to join Baker on the road with the Ellington band in Chicago.

We can only imagine what Mary's first band sounded like since the sextet never recorded. On the surface this seems especially baffling, as Hammond worked for Columbia Records. Yet even if she had wanted to do so, Mary could not have recorded in 1943. The previous summer, in an attempt to assist musicians whose live performances were being replaced by radio and jukeboxes, the American Federation of Musicians (AFM) had instituted a ban prohibiting its members from making recordings. The union wanted record companies to pay royalties on record sales, which would then go toward hiring live musicians. When labels refused to pay, they could not record any new music. The ban, which coincided with Mary's entry into the New York jazz scene, lasted for almost two years.

By leaving New York to travel with Baker on tour, Mary was walking away from performance opportunities and making herself financially dependent on her husband. Louise Crane, the agent who had booked her at Kelly's Stable, insisted that Mary pay her $1,300 in lost revenue. Having no income, Mary wrote to Joe Glaser, asking for a loan. After chastising her, Glaser helped her make a payment plan to Crane in exchange for a release from her contract. He also offered to book dates for Mary if she would leave Baker, inferring that marriage between two competitive musicians would hinder Mary's solo career. But Mary did the opposite and married Baker on a tour stop in Washington, DC, on December 10, 1942. In just a few months' time, she became a staff arranger for Ellington, the first new arranger he had chosen to work with since hiring Billy Strayhorn in 1939.

After six months on the road, Mary made a permanent move to New York in the summer of 1943, finding a small one-bedroom apartment at 63 Hamilton Terrace in the Sugar Hill section of Harlem. Her apartment was simple and bright, her first home since beginning her life as a touring musician almost twenty years earlier. She painted her kitchen yellow and had two pink twin beds in the bedroom, where she would compose music and write letters. She outfitted her living room, which became the center of nighttime musical salons, with a Baldwin upright piano and a small white rug where friends would sit and listen to records. While Mary wanted to provide a home for both herself and her husband, Baker never stayed at the apartment: after being drafted into the military, the couple's relationship faded. While they never divorced, Baker and Mary did not see each other for years.

Although Mary was making a permanent home for herself where she would welcome friends and musicians for decades, her first days in Harlem were filled with the sights and sounds of unrest in the streets. Over the course of two days in August 1943, Harlem was engulfed by riots that saw hundreds arrested, over $5 million in damages to looted businesses, and six people dead. The African American newspaper the *New York Amsterdam News* published a photo of the Braddock Hotel at the corner of 126th Street and Eighth Avenue with the caption, "WHERE IT STARTED . . . it was in the lobby of this hotel where a white policeman shot a Negro soldier in the back Sunday night. This incident . . . turned many Harlemites into hoodlums and vandals who literally wrecked the community."[1] Police officer James Collins had been about to arrest a woman at the Braddock for "profane language" when Private Robert Bandy grabbed Collins's nightstick, beating him over the head. While Bandy was running out of the hotel, Collins shot him in the shoulder, placed him under arrest, and took him to Sydenham Hospital "with a crowd following."[2] A rumor spread that Collins had killed Bandy, starting a chain reaction of residents pouring into the streets, including a group of 3,000 that formed outside the 123rd Street police precinct. Mayor Fiorello LaGuardia and NAACP president Walter White, who were driven through Harlem in police cars, appealed to citizens to go home. A "riot list of the injured and dead" included names of some fifty residents who had been stabbed, shot, bitten, or cut by bricks or bottles.[3]

The riots were just one example of how Harlem was beginning to be seen as unsafe, especially by white New Yorkers. Over the previous decade, Mary's fans had come to Harlem to hear her perform with Andy Kirk at venues like the Savoy Ballroom, but the neighborhood was no longer the center of the city's jazz scene. While this change was partially due to a shift from dancing to jazz at Harlem ballrooms to listening to the music in small clubs on 52nd Street, it was exacerbated by the actions of city officials. Mayor La Guardia had closed the Savoy in the spring of 1942, claiming it was a "base for vice"[4] and citing supposed statistics of soldiers who had contracted venereal diseases from women they met at the ballroom. Because the Savoy was a rare venue where audiences and dancers were racially mixed, many claimed that LaGuardia was attempting to segregate gatherings of New Yorkers.

Mary soon began to perform at a rare club where people of different races mixed freely. In 1938, a former shoe salesman from Trenton, New Jersey, named Barney Josephson founded Café Society, a Greenwich Village basement club. Started as an alternative to venues that were segregated both on and off the bandstand, the club was also a "political cabaret" where singer Billie Holiday made history by debuting "Strange Fruit," the haunting protest song about Black lynchings, in 1939. John Hammond, Josephson's artistic advisor, had tried for years to convince Mary to play there. Although she was nervous to perform in a trio setting without the support of a large ensemble like the Clouds, Mary set aside her anxiety and began an unlimited engagement at Café Society on July 6, 1943. Performing three sets nightly at 8, 10:30, and 1 a.m., she drew a large following and was immediately welcomed into the venue's artist community comprised of singers Holiday and Josh White, pianists Hazel Scott and Teddy Wilson, dancer Pearl Primus, and trumpeter Frankie Newton. The artist-heavy audience often included singer-activist Paul Robeson and artist David Stone Martin, who became a close friend.

Although she received critical accolades, reporters often pitted Mary against Scott, the Trinidadian-born pianist who later became a spiritual companion to Mary. A *Time* magazine review of Mary's Café Society debut entitled "No Kitten on the Keys" opened with, "If you shut your eyes you would bet she was a man. But last week's audiences . . . had their eyes open. They heard a sinewy young Negro woman play the solid, unpretentious, flesh-&-bone kind of jazz piano that is expected from such vigorous Negro masters as James P. Johnson . . . Mary Lou Williams was not selling a pretty face, or a low décolletage, or tricky swinging of Bach or Chopin. She was playing blues, stomps and boogie-woogie."[5] The writer is obliquely comparing Mary with Scott, who three years prior had made a "swinging the classics" record and was often referred to solely in terms of her sex appeal. Even Josephson encouraged Mary to be more coquettish in her audience interactions, thinking this would make her a bigger star. But Mary, steadfastly focused on being taken seriously as a musician, refused. Although she had already made her reputation as "the lady who swings the band" with Andy Kirk, when Mary stepped out on her own, the strength of her playing was not "expected."

While the press may have fabricated a rivalry between Mary and Scott, the two women became good friends. In the fall of 1945, Mary was Scott's bridesmaid at her wedding to Adam Clayton Powell Jr., the New York congressman and pastor of Harlem's Abyssinian Baptist Church. With Scott taking a hiatus from performing, Mary replaced her at Josephson's second club, Café Society Uptown. Through her residency at both venues, Mary gave many benefit performances for politicians. In October 1943, pianist Teddy Wilson curated the entertainment for the "All Star Victory Show," a benefit for city council candidate Benjamin Davis. The headliners included Mary, Billie Holiday, Paul Robeson, Count Basie, and Ella Fitzgerald. Mary also performed in support of President Franklin Delano Roosevelt in the "FDR Victory Bandwagon," traveling with the revue and composing "The Ballot Box Boogie in the Key of Franklin D." While Mary did not explicitly endorse specific candidates, she understood the importance of political involvement, saying, "There's not one musician . . . [who] would be in any kind of political anything if they weren't disturbed about the race . . . [and] trying to help the poor."[6] Mary simply felt that she could do more good on a one-to-one basis. Empathizing with the pain she saw in her neighborhood, she began making "expeditions of mercy"[7] by giving food to neighbors and musicians in need. Susan Reed, a zither player who witnessed one of Mary's quiet acts of charity, said: "I learned a lot about life from Mary. She would never gossip. She spoke very little, but what she said was right on. She said what she meant. When a musician would come to Uptown Café Society and they weren't working that week, I've seen her hand over her pay envelope, the whole envelope, to them. Not say a word."[8]

* * *

In addition to her club performances, Mary began reaching new fans via sheet music and radio. Beginning with his monthly piano column in 1937 in the jazz magazine *Down-Beat*, pianist-critic Sharon Pease began transcribing Mary's music for publication, including an excerpt of her blues composition "Drag 'Em" in his first column. Pease had co-composed Mary's 1938 hit "Ghost of Love" and was one of several transcribers for sheet music publishers who produced folios with titles such as "Boogie-Woogie Piano Styles" or "Mary Lou Williams Boogie-Woogie Piano Transcriptions" so that amateur players could play Mary's music at home. Families without a piano most certainly had a radio. Without new recordings to play on the air due to the recording ban, stations began to feature more live performances. In April 1945, Josephson secured Mary her own half-hour weekly show on New York radio station WNEW. *The Mary Lou Williams Piano Workshop* aired every Sunday at 6 p.m. and featured Mary with her regular trio mates, Al Lucas on bass and Jack "The Bear" Parker on drums.

Josephson's goal in booking Mary on WNEW was not just to increase her audience: he wanted to support Mary's idea for a new, large-scale composition. Mary wanted to create a twelve-part suite based on the signs of the zodiac, with each movement dedicated to a different musician or popular figure who was born under that particular sign. Appropriately, Mary's initial broadcast run was slated for twelve weeks so that she could debut one section each week. She had already improvised three movements at Café Society and had recorded one of them as "Taurus Mood" in March 1944. Searching for a company to record the complete *Zodiac Suite*, Mary turned to record label owner Moe Asch, for whom she had recorded the previous year. Asch gave her complete creative control not only regarding her musical material but also in terms of her cover art. For her earlier album artwork, she had introduced Asch to artist David Stone Martin, who now created a cover with astrological designs in a horseshoe-shaped swirl above a small upright piano.

On June 29, 1945, Mary went into the studio with Al Lucas and Jack Parker. Her original liner notes listed each movement's dedicatees: "Aries" was for the "changeable, moody, and impulsive" Billie Holiday and Ben Webster, while "Taurus" was for Duke Ellington, boxer Joe Louis, and singer Bing Crosby, all "lovers of the arts." Mary closed with a personal statement: "As a composer and musician, I have worked all my life to write and develop serious music that is both original and creative. The *Zodiac Suite* is the beginning of a real fulfillment of one of my ambitions."[9] Each two- to three-minute movement straddles classical and jazz, sounding at times like Ravel or Debussy and at other moments foreshadowing developments in bebop, the incipient new movement in jazz. The record was named as one of *Metronome*'s albums of the year and more than fifty years later was inducted into the 2020 Grammy Hall of Fame.

In addition to the trio recording, Mary created two orchestral versions of the *Zodiac Suite*, first for a chamber orchestra and eight-piece jazz combo on December 31, 1945, at Town Hall and for the seventy-piece Carnegie Pops Orchestra in July of 1946. Press reviews for both performances were mixed, but Barry Ulanov offered a balanced perspective in *Metronome*: "Credit Mary Lou Williams with a brave try, a partial success and the courage of her musical convictions. Her concert at Town Hall . . . was, in spite of many lapses, a handsome demonstration of the music she believes in and I believe in, the music of the future."[10] As one of the first African American jazz musicians to present concert music in typically classical halls, and as her first attempt in composing for strings, Mary had made a pioneering accomplishment. Ten years later, trombonist-composer Melba Liston arranged Mary's "Virgo," "Libra," and "Aries" for the Dizzy Gillespie Orchestra at the 1957 Newport Jazz Festival. Mary also made initial plans with Liston to create a new version of the work for her close friend and fellow pianist Thelonious Monk. Scores in the Liston archives include musical sketches for a project called "Thelonious Monk Plays the *Zodiac Suite*" featuring Monk's quintet with woodwinds, trumpets, French horns, and trombones.[11]

While this new version never came to fruition, it is a reminder that if Mary was playing the *Zodiac Suite* today, she would be creating entirely new versions of the work.

Mary's friendship with Monk was one of many she developed with innovative musicians in the 1940s. Since 1942, players such as saxophonist Charlie "Bird" Parker and trumpeter John Birks "Dizzy" Gillespie had been developing bebop, a new style of jazz that relied on the virtuosity of individual soloists and was executed at tempos too fast for the average dancer. Many older swing era big band musicians did not welcome the new style. But Mary, who always viewed herself as an experimenter, was intrigued with this new era. After finishing her Café Society sets, she would sit in at Minton's Playhouse—the club on 118th Street that was an incubator for beboppers such as Monk, Parker, and Gillespie—to try out new ideas. They continued their experimentations at Mary's apartment, with Monk bringing new compositions for Mary's feedback, seeking her input before performing them in public.

While Mary was not touted as a bebop musician, Dizzy, Bird, and Monk—all three credited as the founders of bop—acknowledged her as having pioneered elements of the style before it officially existed. Mary herself commented that she was using "bop chords" in the early 1940s—chords that would show up in Monk's compositions in the 1950s. Most famously, Monk borrowed a snippet of Mary's 1936 hit "Walkin' and Swingin'" in the first four bars of his 1957 composition "Rhythm-a-Ning." All of the musicians who came to Mary's apartment viewed her as both a mentor and colleague. Mary, in turn, fostered a community reminiscent of her Andy Kirk days, where musicians were finding new sounds and developing a close camaraderie. In the 1947 article "Music and Progress," Mary explained her philosophy:

"If we are to make progress in modern music, or, if you prefer, *jazz*, we must be willing and able to open our minds to new ideas and developments. . . . Be-bop is certainly the most influential and important development that jazz has known for many years. I believe that all musicians should open their minds to it in order to understand what it means to them and to their music."[12]

* * *

In the late summer of 1946, Mary took an extended break from public performance. Having spent over a year composing, arranging, and performing the *Zodiac Suite*, she wanted to take time to get to know her neighborhood. On evening walks, Mary now saw a side to Harlem that was only hinted at during the daytime, with gangs, heroin, and blocks that had been forever affected by the 1943 riots. While her apartment was robbed many times beginning in the 1940s all the way through the 1960s, Mary now began robbing herself by indulging in gambling. She had enjoyed playing cards with the Clouds, but now, visiting nightly card games, Mary began losing money. She confessed, "My name was ringing all over Harlem as the poker chump."[13] Mary began making frequent bank withdrawals to cover her losses that she "stopped counting at $7,000."[14] As scholar Farah Jasmine Griffin observed, "Sitting in on card games the way she used to sit in with musicians, Mary came to a conclusion about the city: 'New York is a town [where] if one takes a vacation or relaxes and tries to be normal and nice something happens. To explore New York means certain death. . . . One has to be tough and on the alert.' "[15]

Mary found temporary salvation from gambling by working to save others. She began visiting sick musicians, cooking and doing laundry for them, and even began bringing musicians who struggled with heroin addiction into her home. Believing in the power of music to save lives, she played music for her houseguests and offered to give free concerts at area public schools. After several months, she had lost so much of her own money that she finally returned to performing, taking touring gigs that Joe Glaser booked for her and playing at Café Society when in New York.

Even during her hiatus, Mary occasionally recorded. In 1946, producer Leonard Feather formed an all-female quintet including Mary on piano for the Continental record label. The session was successful enough that RCA Victor decided to release an album of 78s entitled *Girls in Jazz* featuring several all-female groups. Out of the thirteen tracks that Mary recorded over the course of three sessions, one stands out. Her original composition "Waltz Boogie" mixed elements of boogie-woogie, a waltz feel, and bebop in a single piece, something that had never been done before in jazz. But while the recording made a "best albums of the year" list in the January 1948 issue of *Metronome*, it did not lead to major recording offers for Mary's regular trio.

It is ironic that while Mary experienced success at Café Society until the late 1940s and was revered by bebop musicians, she never saw the commercial recording success that musicians like Monk, Blakey, Bird, or Dizzy received. For all of her brilliance as a forward-thinking, breathtakingly original pianist and composer, Mary was still "seen" as a female musician in the public eye. Unlike those of her male colleagues, Mary's compositions are unknown to most professional jazz musicians outside of the *Zodiac Suite*. Instead, Mary is lauded for being a matronly figure who mentored Monk and Dizzy at her nightly musical salons. Her pieces like "Waltz Boogie" are not performed or known. And although musicians frequently borrowed from each other in their compositions, it is Monk who is most often credited as being the composer of the modern jazz standard "Hackensack," first recorded in 1954 when, in fact, the tune's theme was identical to the melody on Mary's arrangement of the George Gershwin standard "Lady Be Good" from her 1944 recording.

Mary ended the 1940s facing a lawsuit from trombonists Lawrence "Snub" Mosley and Bill Johnson, both of whom wanted co-composer credit for "Pretty Eyed Baby," a piece from one of Mary's 1944 recordings that had started off as "Satchel Mouth Baby." Mosley had added a lyric and Johnson added a coda, both after Mary's original release. Since Mary had neglected to file her work with the copyright office, she lost the battle and was forced to split royalties three ways.

Mary's compositions such as "Waltz Boogie" are still waiting to be discovered by contemporary jazz musicians. Just like her unsatisfying resolution to the "Pretty Eyed Baby" lawsuit, her legacy is still waiting to receive credit where credit is due.

CHAPTER FOUR

Restless and Revolutionary
(1952–54)

> Mary Lou Williams was a seeker-musician, a musician-seeker. Wherever she was, she was always probing, looking for more, and marvelously finding it.
>
> —Barry Ulanov, interview in *Music on My Mind*, directed by Joanne Burke

After living in New York for almost a decade, Mary made her first trip to Europe in November 1952 to headline "The Big Rhythm Show," a variety show that was booked on a two-week concert tour of England. Traveling across the Atlantic was not an easy thought for Mary: she had a fear of flying and would have to travel by steamer, a five-day journey. Not knowing any English musicians, she was concerned about finding suitable bassists and drummers for the tour. In addition, the timing of the trip meant she would miss visiting family at Christmas. Joe Marsolais, the New York agent who offered Mary the tour, assured her that she could come home on December 28 after her final concert.

When Mary insisted that she have a return ticket in hand before setting sail, Marsolais refused, saying that an English booking agency would provide her ticket once she arrived. This, however, turned out not to be the case.

What was supposed to be a two-week tour turned into a two-year sojourn, and marked the beginning of a sea change in Mary's life. Having never been to England, Mary wasn't aware of the country's jazz-loving public that adored her music or the recording companies that were eager to work with her. Mary's first recording for the Vogue label would generate heated debate in the pages of *Melody Maker*, the English jazz magazine that published a three-month serial of her autobiography in 1954. This level of notoriety—something Mary had rarely received Stateside—allowed her to be "seen" as the brilliant jazz musician she was. Yet it was also in Europe, while surrounded by expatriate American artists in Paris, where Mary began to question her vocation. Perhaps as she reflected on her life story for *Melody Maker*, Mary was unconsciously doing a form of the Ignatian Examen, looking back to discern when she had felt closest to God and when she felt furthest away. Spending more and more time in isolation, she realized at the age of forty-four that she "had never reached God."[1] Mary's time in Europe marked the start of her interior seeking, a "dark night of the soul" that offered no way out but *through*.

* * *

On the afternoon of November 28, 1952, Mary boarded the *Queen Elizabeth* for England. Docking five days later at Southampton, she anxiously waited in an unheated station for Harry Dawson, the English agent who had booked her concert dates, to drive her the seventy miles to London. When

Dawson finally arrived, he was missing one item: Mary's return ticket. Mary's misgivings were somewhat quelled by the warm reception she received from a small, devoted group of fans on arriving in London. At a party given in her honor, Mary met other musicians with whom she would be sharing the same bill. She now realized that, unlike what she had been promised, she was not the main attraction of "The Big Rhythm Show." Instead, she was to share headliner status with Cab Calloway and dancer-singer Marie Bryant. Although she was disappointed, she had no choice but to fulfill her concert obligations. Reviews of Mary's December 7 debut at the Royal Albert Hall praised her playing. Critic Max Jones, a writer for *Melody Maker* who became an important friend to Mary, wrote that her playing was "nothing less than a revelation. It is the overall impact of her greatness that is quite overwhelming."[2]

Mary did not love England at first sight. Neither her accommodations nor the food were to her taste, and an intense fog meant that several concert dates were rescheduled, extending her trip. She was still without a return ticket and learned that Dawson was unable to pay some of the musicians. Mary had to be threatened with a lawsuit to show up for the final concert on January 11, 1953, where she shared the stage with pianist Lil Hardin Armstrong. Yet even with these mounting frustrations, Mary realized she was receiving more of a critical response in England than in New York, and so decided to extend her stay.

Weeks before she had left New York, a critic had written that "the trouble with Mary Lou is she hasn't got a definite style." Confronted with the comment, Mary replied, "I consider that a compliment, although I think anyone with ears can identify me without any difficulty. But it is true that I'm always experimenting, always changing, always finding new things."[3] Mary turned what was meant to be critical into a badge of honor, often stating proudly that no one could "pin a style" on her. After recording her first session for the London-based Vogue label in January 1953, Mary's new "modern" style generated similar debate in the pages of *Melody Maker*. Critic Mark Nevard wrote, "It's 100 percent in the modern idiom, and, after all, a lot of us pay homage to the girl pianist who spans a decade, moves with the times, and all that. But when you listen to the record with the history stripped off it just adds up to a listless string of notes."[4] A flood of comments from critics, musicians, and fans poured in. Edgar Jackson defended Mary, writing, "Nevard stresses Mary Lou's lack of emotion but fails to point out that this is characteristic of the 'cool' trend in jazz. Also she has originality, tastefulness and general appeal, which seem to have been lost on Mike."[5] British pianist Dill Jones, whom Nevard had mentioned as being a superior player to Mary, chimed in, "Mary Lou plays more music on one side than I could on twenty."[6] Vogue began to advertise the record as the "most controversial album of the year," garnering Mary more performance invitations.

In March, Max Jones offered Mary the chance to tell the story of her thirty-year career in *Melody Maker*. Based on three weeks of interviews, and using only Mary's words, "Mary Lou Williams: My Life with the Kings of Jazz" was published in eleven installments from April through June of 1954. The articles remain the best way to learn about the first half of Mary's life from her perspective and, thankfully, appear in the 1999 critical anthology *Reading Jazz*.[7]

After spending almost a year in England, in November 1953 Mary moved to Paris. She had already performed in the city on several tours and had friends there, including Don Byas and Hazel Scott. In the 1940s and 1950s, many African

American artists either moved to or spent extended time in France, finding more opportunity in a country where race was not a barrier to commercial success. Mary made her new home on the Left Bank at the barebones Hotel Cristal where writer James Baldwin and singer-dancer Eartha Kitt also lived. Her performances at the Perdido Club became so popular that the club was renamed "Chez Mary Lou."

In December, Mary made her second recording for Vogue with Don Byas, bassist Buddy Banks, and a young Parisian drummer, Gérard "Dave" Pochonet. Mary sounds relaxed and in her element on a set that highlights the intricacy of her bop-flavored compositions on "O.W." (dedicated to saxophonist Orlando Wright) and "N.M.E." (for the European jazz magazine, *New Musical Express*). Although the record did not become well known in the States, the quartet session is a high watermark in Mary's recorded output.

While artistically Mary sounded as brilliant as ever during this period, emotionally she struggled with exhaustion that was only exacerbated by her financial situation. Attracted to Parisian couture, Mary often overspent for her performance wardrobe, in one instance facing down creditors over 60,000 francs that she owed for a new dress. An American expatriate named Colonel Edward L. Brennan came to the rescue and paid Mary's debt. A devout Roman Catholic, Brennan must have sensed Mary's restlessness and took her to a small church with a fenced-in garden. Mary began frequenting this quiet spot to pray and reflect on her life, and later told close friends that it was here that she saw a vision of the Virgin Mary. Around the same time, she had another encounter that marked the beginnings of her spiritual search. Playing at a party in England for members of the British royal family, Mary, who never had much to drink, consumed three scotches. Noticing that she appeared upset, a soldier approached her and suggested that she read Psalm 91 for comfort. Over the course of two days, Mary read not just the ninety-first psalm but all 150 of the psalms and experienced a calm as she read.

In May 1954, the death of a friend precipitated what became a full-blown spiritual crisis for Mary. Garland Wilson, a boogie-woogie and stride pianist originally from West Virginia, had become one of Mary's closest friends since she arrived in England. Wilson followed Mary when she moved to Paris, often sharing her small hotel room after their gigs. He played regularly at Le Boeuf sur le Toit (literally, "the ox on the roof," named after a ballet by Jean Cocteau and composer Darius Milhaud), an underground gay club that featured live jazz. Wilson had struggled with ill health throughout his time in Paris. Although Mary had begun to isolate herself from her friends, including Wilson, she was shocked when she received word that he had collapsed at Le Boeuf and died of an internal hemorrhage. The club's manager asked if Mary would take Wilson's place. Mary later recalled, "I asked him, 'Why me?' And he said, 'Because I looked in this billfold and he was carrying your photo next to his heart.' "[8] A friend from Harlem, pianist Aaron Bridgers, filled in for a week until Mary felt ready to start with a new trio she formed with Gérard "Dave" Pochonet. Even though she resumed performing, Mary began to question why she was playing at all. She later described, "I was in my hotel room all alone and all of a sudden it felt like everything I had done up to then meant absolutely nothing. . . . Even my beloved music, the piano I played, all seemed to have lost their appeal. . . . There was no feeling for me to end it all. It was just despondency based on the fact that I felt everything I had been doing was no good."[9]

Pochonet, who had fallen in love with Mary, noticed her depression. Wanting to help, he offered her a place to stay with him at his grandmother's home in Vaucresson, twenty minutes by train from Paris. Mary accepted and moved from her city hotel to the countryside, where she spent her days praying, eating, and sleeping. In the evenings, she took the train with Pochonet into Paris to work at Le Boeuf, but in August 1954, she decided to leave the club for good. In the many retellings of her story that she gave in interviews in the 1960s and 1970s, Mary explained that she simply walked off the stage during a performance and never returned. But according to Aaron Bridgers, the reality was much less dramatic. Knowing that she needed to make a change, Mary sat down with the manager and explained that she needed to leave. She was released from her contract and began renewing her efforts to raise enough money to return to the States, even contacting Joe Marsolais and Harry Dawson asking for her return fare. Both agents declined Mary's request as she had overstayed her initial contract by almost two years.

By the fall, Mary felt well enough to tour with vocalist Sarah Vaughan and saxophonists Coleman Hawkins and Illinois Jacquet. On her return to Paris, Pochonet asked her to marry him. Mary refused, explaining that she was still technically married to Harold Baker and that filing for divorce was too much of an expense. Having finally received enough money from friends to cover her remaining debts and a ticket home, on December 15, 1954, Mary departed for New York. She would not return to Europe for fourteen years.

Mary had already begun to withdraw from the world, but for the next three years, she would retreat in earnest. Not seeing how she could follow the stirrings in her heart that she had begun to experience in prayer and silence while still following her path as a musician, she decided to abandon the path that had been her life for the last forty years. She did not know if she would ever return to music or to Europe again.

CHAPTER FIVE

Reaching the Right Sound (1954–58)

> The grace for playing was out of me. I just couldn't reach the right sound.
>
> —Mary Lou Williams, quoted in Tom O'Leary, "That's Entertainment," *The Monitor* (February 9, 1962)

Mary arrived back in New York in December 1954 with an obsession to save the jazz community, her Harlem neighborhood, and her family. Before leaving Paris, she had two visions. The first forewarned of Charlie "Bird" Parker's death. Mary urgently felt she needed to get home to save him as well as other musicians who were struggling with drug addiction. Speaking to music critic John S. Wilson in 1973, she explained, "I was born a psychic person. . . . I put that in my music . . . if I was playing with any musician on earth, it could be Charlie Parker, I could . . . hear most of the time the next note they're going to make . . . after I stopped playing then my vision and everything went on the outside of music and I began to hear what was going to happen . . . while I was praying. Like I saw Charlie Parker's death."[1]

Just three months after returning home, Mary received a call from her half brother Jerry Burley. Jerry was concerned for Parker: he had seen him leaving Harlem Hospital in subzero weather with sneakers on and asked if Mary could help. Mary called Parker and he promised to drop in on her in the next couple of days. But before he could make the visit, he died at the home of Baroness Pannonica de Koenigwater (nicknamed Nica), a jazz patron and friend of many musicians. Parker's death convinced Mary more than ever that nightclubs—venues where heroin was readily available—were evil places filled with "bad sounds."

Mary's second vision had concerned "a strange foreign sound [that] would enter into . . . jazz and would destroy the heritage, would destroy jazz completely."[2] A decade later, Mary would rail against "avant-garde music" and rock and roll, which she felt was erasing the history of jazz for young people. Now in 1954, Mary was witnessing how a new school of jazz called "cool" or "West Coast" was creating factions within the jazz community. A style made popular most famously by pianist Dave Brubeck, cool jazz reacted to the intricate solos and breakneck speeds of bebop with more relaxed tempos and mellow instrumentation, reflecting the California laid-back feel of its origins. While bebop had celebrated the abilities of improvisers such as Parker and Dizzy Gillespie in small combos, cool jazz emphasized the skills of composer-arrangers to create complex pieces for large ensembles. On the East Coast, musicians including Art Blakey and pianist Horace Silver were playing "hard bop," itself a reaction to cool jazz with its blues and gospel influences, hard-swinging tempos, and emphasis on emotion. Mary's playing, with her always experimental style, did not fit into either category. While she had inspired bebop musicians in the 1940s, now in the mid-1950s Mary did not see a place for herself on the musical scene.

Mary also missed the camaraderie that had once filled her evenings when musicians traversed 52nd Street, playing a gig and walking two doors down to play at the next. By the mid-1950s, the street's long block from 5th to 6th Avenues had morphed from jazz clubs to burlesque clubs. At home, Mary missed her after-hours musical salons, informal gatherings that re-created the sense of community she had cherished during her long tenure in Andy Kirk's band. Wondering what lay in store for jazz as an art form and for musicians who struggled with underemployment or heroin addiction, Mary began to search for meaning in her own life by trying to save her neighbors and family members.

* * *

Returning to her efforts of a decade earlier when she had begun her "expeditions of mercy"[3] to care for musicians in need, Mary decided to use her apartment as a halfway house. She brought drug addicts into her home, fed and clothed them, and gave them a place to sleep. Yet while Mary was completely devoted to helping others, her meager $300 quarterly royalty checks were not enough to sustain both herself and her charitable cases. Concerned about Mary, Dizzy Gillespie and his wife, Lorraine, sent baskets full of food to her doorstep, dispatching their cousin Marion "Boo" Frazier to make the deliveries.

Mary's crusade to save the world extended to her family. While visiting relatives in Pittsburgh, she decided to help her younger half sister Grace Mickles, a pregnant single mother who struggled with alcoholism. For Mary, this meant lugging Grace's entire family—her four children and one grandchild—back to New York to live with her. The undertaking did not go well from the start: while driving back to Manhattan, the family suffered a car accident and Mary's face was cut by glass.

Mary and Grace had never been close. Now in a small apartment with a family of seven, the sisters' relationship became combative. After Mary spent all the income from her royalty checks on her family's needs, she found Grace a job. But Grace was unable to keep the job, spent her welfare checks on alcohol, and lashed out at Mary. After a year, Mary took the family back to Pittsburgh, but this move was just a temporary fix. Mary's need to save everyone around her, especially her nephew Robbie, led to many more extended family stays in her apartment.

The chaos in Mary's home echoed her own internal mental state. She continued having visions of spirits that wanted to destroy jazz and referred to Satan in her diary as "the man . . . madly hustling for souls."[4] But she also found solace in praying and reading the Psalms, which she said "cooled" her.

Remembering the peace she had experienced in Paris during her vision of the Blessed Mother, Mary began searching for a church to offer rest for her soul. She visited Abyssinian Baptist Church on West 138th Street, where Hazel Scott's first husband, Adam Clayton Powell Jr., was pastor. With its membership of over 14,000, Abyssinian was one of the largest Protestant churches in the world. Many artists, including Mary's early idol Thomas "Fats" Waller, had been associated with the congregation. But Mary stayed at Abyssinian for only a few months, not finding the calm she sought.

Even without a spiritual community, Mary persisted in her one-woman charitable efforts, continuing to house musicians who were strung out on heroin—including her close friend, pianist Bud Powell. She sold her $400 designer gowns for $50, not seeing the need for performance clothes. Her entire wardrobe eventually consisted of one dress and one pair of shoes. And while giving up food may have procured some spiritual benefits, Mary fasted for financial reasons, subsisting on water and apples for up to nine days at a time.

* * *

Mary often referred to 1954–57 as a three-year season when she gave up music. It was not the first time she had left scenarios she found unbearable: she had quit her Paris engagement at Le Boeuf sur le Toit, abandoned a recording session with Benny Goodman's quintet in 1948, and left the Clouds in 1942 after ten years on the road. Yet when asked why she left the jazz scene in the mid-1950s, Mary replied, "I didn't really stop on my own. Something carried me away; I began praying and I never thought about playing anymore. I just thought about helping people. . . . I decided to help them in flesh instead of playing for them."[5]

Mary struggled with whether or not to accept occasional work offers. After saying yes to performing at the Hickory House, the club that had cemented a solid reputation for pianist Marian McPartland, she changed her mind and canceled the engagement. Her fear of returning to club environments was exacerbated by seeing friends have their lives destroyed by heroin. Yet even while sidestepping performance offers, Mary did not give up music. In March 1955, she recorded *A Keyboard History*, a trio album that featured the beginnings of her "history of jazz" program, which would become an integral fixture of her concerts in the late 1960s. And at home, Mary claimed to have achieved success in getting two musicians off dope with her prescription of "prayers and music," composing music for her houseguests to play in order to keep their minds off drugs.

Mary needed spiritual sustenance to fuel her daily heroism and observed that other artists were turning to religion. Laurence "Baby Laurence" Jackson, a dancer-singer whom Mary accompanied on Harlem sidewalks, "was snatching people off the street baptizing."[6] Her former bandmate Art Blakey was converting to Islam. Bobbie Ferguson, Mary's niece, recalls seeing a book on Buddhism that Mary was reading,[7] though Mary never referred to the religion. And while her initial churchgoing had not brought the calm that she sought, Mary was about to find another church that would point her toward the Catholic faith.

* * *

In 1956, Mary walked into a church located just a few blocks from her apartment. With its doors open during the daytime, Our Lady of Lourdes Church on 143rd Street soon became Mary's second home. Jotting down names of family members and musicians in a small journal that she carried with her, Mary's daily prayer list grew to over 900 names. Mary felt at peace at Our Lady of Lourdes, saying, "It was the only church that I felt good in, [where] I could meditate without vibes hitting me in the head."[8] She continued, "I never even thought about praying . . . until . . . I got a sound, that everybody should pray in the church every day because the world would change and you would encounter . . . a lot of selfishness in the world."[9] Mary believed that her fellow musicians were hearing the same "sound," explaining, "A lot of musicians and dancers became preachers. . . . They must have gotten the same thing."[10]

Mary began attending daily Mass, often praying at all three morning services. Her routine consisted of mornings and afternoons spent at church, interrupted only by a short walk home to make lunch for whoever was currently staying in her apartment. Subsisting on minimal amounts of food and giving up her bed for her houseguests, Mary was, for all practical purposes, living the life of a consecrated woman religious.

* * *

Our Lady of Lourdes had a piano in its basement and was a space where Mary felt comfortable playing. She continued to hear new compositions in her head, reporting, "I'd go down and meditate in that church and hear some crazy arrangements. They come so fast I can't write them."[11] Mary even wrote to the parish priest, Fr. Dolan, offering to play a concert to help raise money for the church's grammar school. Even though the concert did not take place, Lourdes offered Mary a safe place to play and pray.

Mary became an evangelist among musicians, inviting them to church and teaching them how to pray the rosary. While Gillespie and Hazel Scott were supportive, many did not appreciate Mary's zeal. She managed to convince Thelonious Monk and Bud Powell to accompany her to morning Masses beginning at 7 a.m., an ungodly hour for working musicians. To prep Monk for these marathons, Mary drove him to Our Lady of Lourdes to meditate. En route in Mary's Cadillac, Monk asked to make a pit stop. While Mary waited, Monk disappeared and, without telling her, bought and drank a pint of wine. On arriving at Lourdes, he fell down. Mary relayed, "I pulled him up and said, 'Get up, you big ape.' . . . He said he had never been in a church or anything like that before. . . . He thought I was coming because I thought maybe he was going to die, so he went and got this wine and drank it."[12]

Although Mary had found the beginnings of inner peace, after several months she wrote to Fr. Dolan complaining of "strange vibrations" at Our Lady of Lourdes and decided to leave. She continued to pray, read the psalms, and feed the hungry. But Mary needed a guide, someone who understood both her vocation as a musician and her attraction to the Catholic faith. Unbeknownst to Mary, her friend Dizzy Gillespie was about to meet a priest in South America who would become her first spiritual companion.

* * *

While Mary was trying to save her local community, Dizzy was spreading the democracy of jazz to far-flung countries. In March of 1956, the State Department sent his twenty-two-piece band on its first ever "musical ambassadors" tour throughout the Middle East, where they were met with overwhelming enthusiasm. In Athens, the band played for students who had attacked an American embassy just days earlier. Immediately following the concert, the audience stormed the stage, lifting Dizzy on their shoulders and parading him through the crowd. A local newspaper reported, "Greek students laid down rocks and rolled with Diz."[13] Dizzy's musical and diplomatic reputation was well known to Fr. John Crowley, CSsR, a Redemptorist priest originally from Boston stationed in Mato Grosso, Brazil. Traveling to Paraguay to hear Dizzy on his second State Department tour in July of 1956, Fr. Crowley introduced himself to Dizzy and Lorraine. His appearance in the Gillespies' lives came at a moment when each of them was finding their own spiritual path: Lorraine was investigating Catholicism, and Dizzy had recently been introduced to the Bahá'í faith. An avid jazz fan, Fr. Crowley had noticed

Mary's disappearance from the jazz scene and asked Dizzy what had happened to her. Crowley's inquiry sparked a new partnership with the goal of helping Mary find her way back to the stage.

A fourth person soon contributed to the trio's mission to aid Mary. One year earlier, Fr. Crowley had written to Barry Ulanov to renew his lapsed subscription to *Metronome*, the jazz magazine of which Ulanov served as editor. A recent convert to Catholicism and a prolific author on jazz and religion, Ulanov understood Fr. Crowley's twin loves of jazz and the church. While attending Columbia University in the 1930s in order to be close to the Harlem jazz scene, Ulanov became friends with writer Thomas Merton and poet Robert Lax, fellow jazz lovers and students who seriously considered "religion as a way of life."[14]

These four spiritual and musical ambassadors—Fr. Crowley, Dizzy, Lorraine, and Ulanov—all loved Mary. Together they would help her find her way back to music and point her to a Jesuit priest who would become her closest spiritual companion.

* * *

On a visit home in late 1956, Fr. Crowley stopped in New York where Lorraine introduced him to Mary. The occasion marked the first time that Mary had spoken with a priest who understood both her calling as a jazz musician and her need to save others. Crowley advised Mary to stop rehabilitating addicts in her home, suggesting instead that she offer her music as prayer. Deeply moved at seeing her ministry in person, Crowley declared to the Gillespies, "Mary is a saint." He soon brought Mary to Ulanov's West Village home. Mary recalled that Crowley's intentions became overtly clear when he bluntly proclaimed to Ulanov, "'She should be Catholic. Get a priest for her. She wants to be Catholic.' So Barry [Ulanov] said, 'I'll get one of the greatest priests that's ever lived.' He got hold of Father Woods and he was really something else."[15]

Fr. Anthony Woods, SJ, was a Jesuit priest at the Upper East Side St. Ignatius Loyola Church at 84th Street and Park Avenue. A jazz lover and an impassioned civil rights advocate, Woods was introduced to Mary one year before he was appointed as parish priest at the other prominent Jesuit parish in Manhattan, St. Francis Xavier Church, located on West 16th Street in the bohemian neighborhood of Chelsea. While both parishes were (and remain today) inclusive, social justice–minded communities undergirded by lay programs in Ignatian spirituality, their milieus were quite different. Xavier was a hub of Catholic intellectual thought filled with artists, activists, and musical outreach. Woods's sermons pointedly addressed the need for Catholics to fight against racist policies and politicians, and he instituted an annual civil rights Mass at the church in 1960. St. Francis Xavier was also a home for the arts, where conductor Vincent La Selva led an all-volunteer symphony, dubbed "the miracle on 16th Street,"[16] in free performances. Ulanov had founded two discussion groups at the church: the Thomas More Society, a theology group of which Woods served as treasurer; and the Catholic Renascence Society, a literary association whose officers included Fr. Norman Weyand, SJ, and Cardinal John J. Wright, two men who would soon become important allies to Mary. St. Francis Xavier's theology, music, and social action would influence and be influenced by Mary's first liturgical jazz work in 1962.

In contrast to the artist-centric Chelsea neighborhood of St. Francis Xavier Church, St. Ignatius Loyola Church is situated in one of the most affluent, predominantly white neighborhoods in Manhattan. The interior and exterior of St. Ignatius reflects the opulence of its congregation and surrounding community. Its Park Avenue edifice is massive, taking up an entire city block. The church sanctuary ignites the senses with its Tiffany glass, marble, and twelve-panel bronze doors that were gifted to the parish just prior to the Great Depression. It is at St. Ignatius where Mary and Lorraine began taking weekly catechism classes with Fr. Woods in 1957.

Fr. Woods and Mary developed a strong bond of spiritual companionship. Mary valued her time with the priest so much that she walked more than 120 blocks to St. Francis Xavier Church for their sessions when she did not have money to ride the subway. Woods showed Mary how to pray for everyone on her extensive list without individually naming each of her 900 prayer dedicatees. Describing her rare quality of soul, he commented, "She seems to have an understanding of what is good, of what is beautiful. . . . In her uncomplicated way, she can't understand how anybody can't be sincere. To me, she is one of the greatest persons I have ever met."[17] One of Mary's former students, the peace activist Fr. John Dear, recalled, "She [Mary] told me about . . . Woods, coming and telling her very gently that you should ask God not to have visions anymore, so that you can get back to having an ordinary spiritual life, loving people and serving them through music. . . . She's having these visions of the saints—and this Jesuit says there's a deeper thing. I was very taken by it and she was, too."[18]

Just one day after Mary's forty-seventh birthday, on May 9, 1957, she and Lorraine were baptized and received into the Catholic Church in a ceremony at St. Ignatius. Ulanov and his wife, Joan, were present as Mary's sponsors, spiritual companions who were tasked with praying for Mary daily. Mary was now being sustained by a community of Catholics who were about to love her back to the stage.

* * *

Mary's public statement of faith—her baptism—came just two months before her public return to the stage. On July 6, 1957, she played at the Newport Jazz Festival as a featured guest with the Dizzy Gillespie Orchestra. The date marked her first appearance on an American stage in five years, and represented more than three years of encouragement from Dizzy, Fr. Crowley, and Melba Liston, the brilliant trombonist-composer-arranger in Dizzy's band. Liston visited Mary on numerous occasions and relayed her musical praise to Dizzy, saying that Mary "played some chords and you ought to hear them. They're really great."[19] Priests had been very direct with Mary. Fr. Woods advised her, "You're an artist. You belong at the piano and writing music. It's my business to help people through the Church and your business to help people through music."[20] Fr. Crowley counseled, "God wants you to return to the piano. You can serve Him best there for that is what you know best."[21] In the weeks leading up to Newport, Fr. Crowley repeatedly phoned Mary to ensure that she was practicing at least an hour each day.

When the Newport performance finally arrived, Dizzy introduced Mary with deep affection, mentioning two priests in his introduction: Fr. Crowley and Fr. Norman O'Connor, CSP, a festival board member known as "the jazz priest." Dizzy began, "It's very seldom that a great artist that I'm about to present comes on the scene. This young lady has been in semi-retirement for some time now and it was only through the encouragement of Fr. Crowley and Fr. O'Connor and myself that she consented to once again appear on the stage. . . . I'm about to present now, ladies and gentlemen, a truly, truly, truly great artist . . . the dynamic Miss Mary Lou Williams."[22] As Mary walked on stage, Dizzy's band played sixteen bars of her 1948 composition (and the orchestra's theme song), "In the Land of Oo-Bla-Dee," before launching into Liston's new arrangements of "Virgo," "Libra," and "Aries" from Mary's *Zodiac Suite*. Dizzy's bandmates called out their approval during Mary's solos, and the audience responded enthusiastically.

Although Mary's set was recorded and released, Newport did not catapult her back onto the jazz scene or curb her doubts regarding public performance. In a 1958 *Sepia* article entitled "What I Learned from God about Jazz," she wrote, "Although I was received very well [at Newport], I still did not feel I was with it—I mean the music. I just didn't feel it was good."[23] But a month later she accepted an invitation to perform at an East Side club called the Composer. Mary explained, "I suddenly got the desire to play again. It happened . . . at the Composer. . . . I suddenly felt that I had at last reached my highest plane in music, for everyone said I was playing as though inspired. To those who would listen, I told them that the reason I was playing that way was because I had at last found God."[24] The press took notice of Mary's return, hailing her as "still one of the finest jazz musicians who ever sat at a piano."[25] Leading her trio opposite Mary's, pianist Marian McPartland professed her unabashed admiration: "Sometimes you are fortunate enough to work opposite a truly mature, creative musician. . . . There is no feeling of competing except in the highest sense—a wish to inspire others and to be inspired by them—but there is a general air of well-being among the musicians and the other persons there. This is the mood that Mary Lou Williams creates at the Composer every evening. . . . So many persons . . . are coming in droves to welcome her and wish her well."[26] In October, McPartland's trio returned to the Hickory House, where Mary was also offered a booking but turned it down. Seven years later, Mary would finally accept an engagement at the Hickory House, at which time the press would tout her second "return" to the jazz scene.

Having spent so much time away from the public, it was hard for Mary to perform night after night. Shy and not wishing to interact with patrons, she hid in a coatroom between sets. She recalled, "I hadn't been around people in a long time. When I came off the stand [bandstand] I'd run to the checkroom and hide behind the coats. . . . The drummer, Bill Clark, and my bass player, they were running to the checkroom with me after a while."[27] Owner Sy Baron eventually coaxed Mary out of the checkroom, but Mary would "sit in the corner as if I was having a chill. It's just terrible to get away from people six months or a year and then go around them. You're shy and you're withdrawn."[28]

Even though Mary expended her energy in her nightly performances, her run at the Composer was extended to six months, into early 1958. Despite her fear of returning to the stage, she knew that her home was at the piano sharing her music with others. Mary's faith in herself was being strengthened by a larger community of fellow believers in God and in jazz.

CHAPTER SIX

Keep Your Heart High (1958–62)

> There's a funny thing that happens with me, if you really want to see some piano playing or work done, let me know that there's somebody that needs help or there's a condition that exists, and I'll come out and do something. I'm like a big bear then doing it.
>
> —Mary Lou Williams, interview in *Music on My Mind*, directed by Joanne Burke

As a new convert, Mary committed to a daily spiritual practice that went far beyond quietly sitting in a pew, hearing the Mass in Latin, and fingering her rosary beads. Nor did she content herself with privately carrying out acts of mercy. Instead, Mary searched for new ways to extend the sense of community fostered in a nightclub between audience and performers into everyday life. Just as musicians shared love as they gave of themselves in their playing, Mary now sought a way for the public to express their love toward musicians by providing for their practical, physical needs.

* * *

After Charlie Parker's death, Mary served for several months as co-chair of the Charlie Parker Foundation along with Dizzy Gillespie and Hazel Scott. In April 1955, the foundation produced a massive benefit concert at Carnegie Hall with more than thirty-five musicians including Dizzy, Mary, Monk, Billie Holiday, and saxophonist Lester Young. The event raised $10,000 for Parker's children and gave Mary the idea to start her own foundation to assist musicians in need.

After Mary spoke with Fr. Woods about her concert idea, he connected her with lawyer Herbert J. Bliss, who helped incorporate her Bel Canto Foundation in 1958. The nonprofit's mission statement read, "To voluntarily assist in relief of every kind and nature to those persons suffering from or exposed to alcohol or drugs to any degree, but primarily to musicians."[1] Mary's dream included having a home outside of the city staffed with medical personnel where musicians could rest and heal. To raise funds for Bel Canto, she decided to rent Carnegie Hall for a benefit concert. But first, she had to come up with the venue's rental fee. Two of Mary's philanthropist—and billionaire—friends, the arch rivals Doris Duke and Barbara Hutton, gave Mary the necessary financial loans. On September 20, 1958, a gathering of more than sixty jazz musicians including Ben Webster, Hazel Scott, organist Shirley Scott, and drummer Roy Haynes assembled at Carnegie for the "Bel Canto Foundation Jazz Concert to Benefit Musicians." St. Francis Xavier's all-volunteer Xavier Symphony opened the concert with the overture from Leonard Bernstein's *Candide*; boxer Sugar Ray Robinson gave a speech; and Mary performed a new Melba Liston arrangement of her 1937 hit "Roll 'Em." Although the stage was packed, the house was far from full and the benefit concert lost money, leaving Mary unable to pay back her benefactors or cover her expenses. Both Duke and Hutton were not pleased, and Bliss had to convince Hutton to drop a threatened lawsuit against Mary for not paying back her loan. In the meantime, Elaine Lorillard, one of the founders of the Newport Jazz Festival, lent Mary funds to help cover her deficit.

While Mary's friends may have felt she was overreaching in her fundraising efforts, Mary had originally anticipated that a live recording of the concert could also be sold, with all proceeds going to Bel Canto. In order to make a commercial recording with union musicians who were already volunteering their time, Mary had to ask for permission. Bliss contacted Local 802, the New York branch of the American Federation of Musicians, on Mary's behalf, but the union denied Mary's request, as none of the musicians would be receiving financial compensation for the recording.

Undeterred, Mary sent appeals to potential donors, among them the Catholic Worker founder Dorothy Day and pianists Erroll Garner and Dave Brubeck. She attempted to recoup numerous lost royalty payments and pitched concert ideas to Catholic universities with the intention of donating her proceeds to Bel Canto. Although these efforts did not yield much revenue, Mary was succeeding at making a larger community both inside and outside of church aware of the plight of drug-addicted musicians.

No matter her own financial situation, Mary was not going to let a lack of money stop her work. In the fall of 1959, she opened a thrift shop at 308 East 29th Street with all proceeds to go to Bel Canto and toward "loans" to musicians. Enlisting donations from friends, Mary's stock soon included clothing from Saks Fifth Avenue, shoes and ties from Duke Ellington and Dizzy Gillespie, and dresses from Peggy Hitchcock, a cousin of the Mellon family. Mary played at an upright piano for parties in the shop, inviting potential patrons to browse the merchandise. In a May 1964 article in *The New Yorker*, Whitney Balliett described his first impression of the shop: "The walls were covered with paintings by amateurs, whose enthusiasms ranged from Grandma Moses to Picasso. Two handsome evening dresses hung in the windows, and around the shop were odd pieces of china, a sewing machine, a butcher's mallet, a rack of clothes covered with a plastic sheet, a cue stick encased in a fancy scabbard, serving trays, a tin lunchbox, rows and rows of shoes . . . In the back . . . were piles of books and records, and two automobile tires in good condition. Everything was peppered with New York grit."[2]

Mary had kept notebooks of her own daily expenses for years. To satisfy the requirements for a tax-free charity, she filed meticulous bookkeeping records for the shop, trying her best to be present for drop-in visits by the Internal Revenue Service. Besides her time, she consistently invested her own income in the endeavor: as late as 1965, Mary gave her regular salary from a long-running gig at the Hickory House of $512.71 as well as $2,000 from additional performance revenue to cover shop expenses. On top of this, she was giving money to her half sister Grace for daily necessities of food, rent, and bus fare. Mary also practiced tithing, writing checks in the amount of $20 to Our Lady of Lourdes for prayer candles and $400 to the Catholic Youth Organization, and sending donations to places she went to on religious retreats such as the Cenacle sisters in Lancaster, Massachusetts.[3]

On paper, Mary's Bel Canto venture was not self-sustaining and made little sense in terms of dollars and cents. But musicians like Dizzy Gillespie appreciated how much Mary gave to the community, explaining, "As strongly as her devotion to music [was], I think her devotion to humanitarian work was just as strong. So she really helped a lot of musicians, give 'em money, loan 'em money, never paid back. She was great."[4] Mary often gave cash directly to musicians. One of her beneficiaries was the arranger George Gordon, whose vocal group appeared on her 1964 *Black Christ of the Andes* album. Historian Vaughn Booker describes her acts of charity:

> Fifteen dollars (about $125 in 2018 dollars) for George Gordon may not have been enough to cover his healthcare costs, but the relatively insubstantial amount obscures the degree of Williams's actual involvement when she "took care of him" in her shop. Her "care" may have involved constant communication with Gordon over his period of recuperation, errands she may have run for him, recruiting others to check in on his progress, preparing meals for him. . . . The checks may have even represented the official amount that Williams provided Gordon once he was well enough to leave the shop, concealing her unofficial investment of time and finances to ensure his recovery.[5]

For five years, Mary struggled to keep her East Side shop open. Although it closed in the mid-1960s, in 1966 she opened a boutique in Harlem in partnership with restaurateur Joe Wells, again to benefit Bel Canto. While this second shop only lasted for several years, Mary's impact did not go unnoticed. Fr. Norman Weyand, SJ, the chaplain of the Catholic Renascence Society, mentioned Mary's Bel Canto efforts in the September 1964 issue of *Review for Religious*. Reviewing *The Junkie Priest*, a book about Fr. Daniel Egan, SA, a Franciscan who ministered to female drug addicts in New York, Weyand wrote that America needed to follow more "enlightened polices" to handle the issue of narcotics in large cities:

> My own interest in the problem has been sharpened by the death a few years ago of Billie Holiday, the greatest jazz singer our country has produced—and a tragic victim of environment, segregation, prejudice, and our narcotics policies. Billie, thank God, died in the Catholic church. Just recently, too, a meeting with one of our greatest jazz pianists, the Catholic convert Mary Lou Williams . . . emphasized for me the importance of efforts to help our narcotic addicts. Miss Williams' chief expenditure of time, outside of her musical work, is devoted to aiding and rehabilitating musicians addicted to drugs through her Bel Canto Foundation. Religious would do well to include in their prayers and intentions in the Holy Sacrifice people such as Father Egan and Miss Williams and the unfortunate victims whom they are helping with the greatest of self sacrifice.[6]

* * *

Among religious, it was not just the Jesuits who supported Mary's work. Several months prior to opening her first shop, Mary met a Franciscan brother who became a close friend for the next twenty years. Returning home from a concert engagement in Albany, Mary and her sometimes manager Joe Glaser made a stop at Graymoor, a community run by the Franciscan Friars of the Atonement located in Garrison, about fifty miles north of Manhattan in the Hudson River Valley. On entering Graymoor's gift shop, Mary spotted Br. Mario Hancock, SA, a twenty-one-year-old African American who had recently taken his first vows in the Franciscan order. Up to this point, Mary had been surrounded by mostly white Jesuits. Now in her first encounter with a cassock-wearing African American, she plied Br. Mario with questions. Br. Mario later recalled:

> I was in the gift shop when they walked in. She [Mary] was thin then and very pretty, in a dark coat with her hair flowing as usual, and I knew immediately she was an exceptional person, not an ordinary person that makes a pilgrimage. She carried herself like a lady. I thought that Glaser was her husband, but she introduced him as her manager. Joe Glaser seemed in a rush but she was saying, "Wait, wait." She was just bubbling over, overjoyed to see a black religious and she gave me her address and sent Glaser back to the car to get some of her records—some 45s. Then Glaser tried to get across to me how important she was. "She's a very famous jazz pianist."[7]

In the fall, Mary returned to Graymoor to make a private retreat. During her stay, she spent extended time in conversation with Br. Mario. Despite their age difference, the two must have had much to discuss: like Mary, Br. Mario was born in Georgia and moved north (to Newark) with his family as a youngster. Born as Grady Hancock, he took the religious name of Mario when he was received as a Franciscan novice in 1956. Both knew of their vocational callings at an early age. And in their respective Catholic communities, both were in the minority as people of color. Br. Mario would soon play a key role in helping Mary compose her first liturgical jazz and, later, in performing her music in Rome.

Even though Br. Mario and other friends continued to encourage Mary, she was still hesitant to perform regularly and seemed to appear and disappear from the jazz scene like a jack-in-the-box. It was not until 1962, when she accepted an offer from Joe Glaser for a three-month engagement at a San Francisco hotel bar, that Mary stopped retreating from the public eye. To ease her anxiousness, Glaser asked Mary's friend Louis Armstrong, then in California, to check in with her. Besides Armstrong, Mary befriended the local actor Lloyd Bridges on her nightly trio gig with bassist George Tucker and drummer Al Harewood at the Tudor Room inside the Sheraton-Palace Hotel. In the press, a *DownBeat* reviewer bemoaned the fact that the large room's poor acoustics and distracting bar and kitchen noise were not suitable for Mary's San Francisco debut. But he praised the band, saying that "the trio swings from first to last" and that patrons "fortunate enough to obtain a seat near the bandstand were rewarded with some of the most delightful jazz ever heard in this area."[8]

In an interview in the local archdiocesan newspaper *The Monitor,* Mary mentioned a nun who had helped her find her way back to the piano. Reporter Tom O'Leary listed this sister only as "Mother Mulligan, a Cenacle nun who once insisted Mary Lou practice the piano while on a retreat in Mt. Kisco."[9] In the late 1950s, Fr. Woods had contacted Sr. Martha Mulligan at the Cenacle motherhouse in Mount Kisco, New York, to help Mary make what was probably her first spiritual retreat. The Cenacles' stated mission is to surrender their whole lives to God through prayer, community, and spiritual ministry—exactly what Mary had been doing through her music and works of mercy. Beginning with Mary's first visit, the two women became soul friends and wrote consistently to each other for more than seventeen years, often as frequently as every two weeks. In an April 1978 letter to Mary, Sr. Martha recalled, "I was reminded of his [Woods's] phone call to Mt. Kisco asking me to take you on the retreat. He said, 'You know Mary Lou, don't you?'—'No, I never heard of her.'—'Well, you're going to hear a lot about her. She's somebody!' "[10]

Sr. Martha and Mary offered each other mutual encouragement through hard times. In her letters Sr. Martha constantly reminded Mary that she was praying the Memorare—a prayer invoking the Virgin Mary for protection—daily for her and for her Pittsburgh relatives. As Mary began touring more regularly in the late 1960s and 1970s, Sr. Martha implored her to take time to rest and scheduled occasional retreats for her at various Cenacle facilities in the Northeast.

Sr. Martha also relayed her struggles of living in limbo for a year after her longtime home at a Cenacle center in Lancaster, Massachusetts, was slated to be closed. Moving to a large motherhouse in Boston—a city she did not like—Sr. Martha asked when Mary would perform her liturgical music at Boston College, something that Mary eventually did in the mid-1970s. Sr. Martha later spoke of her sister Helen's death and consoled Mary in 1965 after she expressed her sorrow at the death of her beloved spiritual confessor, Fr. Woods. Mary sent Sr. Martha recordings and newspaper clippings covering her performances, which Sr. Martha posted on the sisters' bulletin board and preserved in a scrapbook. Sr. Martha occasionally traveled to Manhattan for Mary's performances and prayed for her in the Cenacle chapel when she was unable to be physically present.

In Sr. Martha's last known letter to Mary in the spring of 1980, just one year prior to Mary's death, her handwriting is noticeably shaky. She apologizes for her penmanship, writing that she can barely hold her pencil because of two recent falls. In many of her letters, she exhorts Mary with the phrase "Keep your heart high!" Mary was strengthened to continue to share her music with the public because of deep friendships with religious like Sr. Martha and Br. Mario. Returning to New York after her San Francisco performances in the spring of 1962, she was about to be strengthened by a seventeenth-century Black saint.

CHAPTER SEVEN

Saint Martin and the Steel City (1962–67)

I'm fighting for the freedom of jazz and for the freedom people hear in it.

—Mary Lou Williams, quoted in Harold V. Cohen, "At Random," *Pittsburgh Post-Gazette* (June 5, 1964)

Back in New York, Mary's friends continued encouraging her to keep performing—and to return to composing. Br. Mario had tried to nudge Mary back to writing music during her stays at Graymoor. Now visiting her in her Harlem apartment, he placed a small statue of Blessed Martin de Porres, the seventeenth-century Afro-Peruvian Dominican brother, on top of Mary's Baldwin upright piano, claiming that de Porres would help her to compose again.

The patron of workers for interracial justice and a popular figure for Black American Catholics, de Porres soon became a central influence in Mary's life. Born as the illegitimate son of a dark-skinned Panamanian mother and a white-skinned Spanish nobleman, de Porres had been shunned by his father because of his skin color. On May 6, 1962, just two days before Mary's fifty-second birthday, newspapers declared "a blow to racism" when de Porres was canonized as the first biracial saint by Pope John XXIII. Fr. John Dear, one of Mary's students at Duke University in the late 1970s, recalled Mary's stories about de Porres, relaying, "She was having visions and she was hearing voices of the saints and Jesus. . . . She'd wake up in the morning and Martin de Porres would be standing at the edge of her bed."[1]

Inspired by de Porres, Mary began composing a work for the new saint and brought a melody to Fr. Woods in search of a lyric. Woods penned a text that drew on popular imagery of de Porres, who was often depicted with a broom and small animals at his feet. Armed with a new lyric, Mary spent the next several months expanding her melody into a large-scale *a cappella* choral setting. It was the first time she had written for chorus since 1948, when she composed "Elijah Under the Juniper Tree" with poet Monty Carr for a sixty-voice choir in Pittsburgh.

Giving her new piece two different titles, "Hymn to Saint Martin de Porres" and "Black Christ of the Andes," Mary premiered the work in a stripped-down solo vocal version with soprano Ethel Fields on de Porres's first feast day of November 3, 1962, at St. Francis Xavier Church. The musical event was part of the parish's civil rights Mass, an annual liturgy that Fr. Woods had instituted. Newspapers covered the Mass with the headlines "Negro Saint's Day Held Blow to Racism"[2] and "St. Martin 'Rebuke' to Racist."[3] In his homily, guest preacher Fr. Walter M. Abbott, SJ, declared that the canonization of St. Martin was "the Church's infallible answer to racists who would be Christians" and quoted from the opening statement of the Second Vatican

Council: "We proclaim that all men are brothers, irrespective of the race or the nation to which they belong." In an interview leading up to the premiere, Mary commented, "I couldn't think of any better way of conveying my thoughts than in this music to a saint who worked for many people."[4]

Eight days later, "Saint Martin" was performed in its full choral version at Philharmonic Hall (now Lincoln Center). But critics were unsure what to do with Mary's new music. Some praised the work, writing, "This was a modern spiritual which managed to commingle pride with something of the sadness that is in the blues."[5] Others did not understand why Mary would compose a piece about a religious subject or attempt to write choral music when her expertise was in instrumental music.

Not waiting for critics or record labels to catch up with her new direction, Mary went into the studio with her trio and the Ray Charles Singers, a professional choir known for their appearances on singer Perry Como's television and radio shows. To conduct the ensemble, Mary hired Howard Roberts, the music director of the Alvin Ailey American Dance Theater. Recording "Saint Martin" and "The Devil," an arrangement of actress-singer Ada Moore's 1955 piece, "The Devil is a Woman," Mary released both works in 1963 on *Jazz for the Soul*, a three-track, 45-inch extended play record (EP) on her new independent label, Mary Records. For promotion, she created a homemade flyer, drawing her profile in crayon next to the phrases "a new concept in sound with 14 voices" and "therapeutic rewards for a tired and disturbed soul."

Wanting to expand her three-track EP into a full long-playing record (LP), Mary approached restaurateur Joe Wells for financial backing to cover studio time and musician fees. She now began writing two new vocal pieces in collaboration with trombonist-arranger Melba Liston: "Anima Christi," a gospel-tinged waltz setting of a prayer attributed to St. Ignatius of Loyola (something she had probably learned with Fr. Woods), and "Praise the Lord," a shuffle that included spoken and sung portions of Psalms 148 and 150 in a preaching sermonette style. To cover vocal duties, Mary contracted The Gordons, a quartet with George Gordon, his sons Richard and George Jr, and daughter Honi, whom Mary would feature often in her liturgical jazz throughout the 1960s and 1970s. Highlights of the eight additional instrumental trio tracks featured Mary's swinging arrangement of the Walter Donaldson tune "My Blue Heaven" and "Dirge Blues," a lament that she dedicated to the recently assassinated President John F. Kennedy. For the cover art, David Stone Martin, Mary's friend from Café Society days, created a simple line drawing of Mary's hands folded in prayer against a pink background. Record producer Moe Asch, now with Folkways Records, reunited with Mary to provide album distribution. Drummer and Mary's former boyfriend from Paris, Gérard "Dave" Pochonet wrote the liner notes, which included Mary's wish that "ten percent of the proceeds from this album will be used for the rehabilitation of sick musicians."[6] Mary called the recording *Mary Lou Williams Presents Black Christ of the Andes* and released the project on Mary Records.

Black Christ of the Andes was released at a time when America needed a musical outlet amid the heaviness of the struggle for civil rights. In liner notes to the album's 2004 reissue, Fr. Peter O'Brien, SJ, explains, "Williams, in placing the words 'Black' and 'Christ' together in the one electrifying phrase 'Black Christ,' unified her own religious belief with the political struggle of the period. . . . It was her civil rights statement in 1963."[7]

Although the American jazz press ignored the record—something inconceivable as it was Mary's first release in nine years—Europe was more receptive: in November of 1967, the French critic Hugues Panassié wrote to Mary informing her that the recording had won the "Grand Prix" prize from the "Academie du Disque Français." In her hometown of Pittsburgh, music critic Phyl Garland praised the album in the *Courier*, commenting, "The music accomplishes a miracle. It makes us feel good inside, automatically creating a desire to be good to others. It is a rare thing so seldom accomplished in music or words and ten thousand sermons could not succeed as well."[8]

While Mary was responding in her music to the tumultuousness of the early 1960s, she saw her local Jesuit parishes responding as well. It is very likely that Mary attended a funeral Mass at St. Ignatius Loyola Church on November 26, 1963, for "the three Johns": Pope John XXIII, who died between the first and second meetings of the Second Vatican Council; President John F. Kennedy, who had been assassinated four days earlier; and Fr. John LaFarge, SJ, founder of the Catholic Interracial Council. LaFarge, who died two days after Kennedy, had been present at Martin Luther King Jr.'s "I Have a Dream" speech at the March on Washington just months earlier. Later, Mary would set part of that speech to music and teach it to youth choirs in Harlem and in Rome.

Mary joined with her fellow Catholics in social justice struggles by getting her record out to as many who would listen and sending it to religious like Sr. Martha Mulligan. With the assistance of feature articles in *The New Yorker* and *Time* magazine, the release found its way to new fans, including Peter O'Brien, a young Jesuit seminarian. A 1964 *Time* article entitled "Jazz: The Prayerful One" featured two photos of Mary: one with her trio at the Hickory House, and one of her in a long, dark coat kneeling at the altar at St. Francis Xavier Church. Once again heralding her "return" to the jazz scene, the piece mentioned Mary's jazz hymn for St. Martin de Porres and her connection with Fr. Woods.[9] O'Brien, who knew Woods from his student days at Xavier High School, was currently studying at Loyola Seminary just north of Manhattan. O'Brien wrote to Mary, asking if she would give him a copy of her new album, and soon came to hear her at the Hickory House. He later recalled his first impression of Mary: "An authoritative African American woman in early middle age sat at the piano, eyes mostly closed, her face registering every nuance in the music she was creating. . . . [She] at times broke into a brief radiant smile. . . . You simply knew that you were in the presence of someone of the highest magnitude. . . . The emotional experience of the music and the woman herself was so strong that my life at once took on a permanent new direction."[10] During a set break, Mary spoke with O'Brien and gave him a copy of *Black Christ of the Andes*. Glad of a new religious companion, especially since Br. Mario had been recently stationed in Rome, Mary and O'Brien developed a fast friendship via daily phone conversations and frequent visits at Mary's apartment. One of Mary's biggest champions, O'Brien would eventually become her full-time manager through a special arrangement with the Jesuits in 1968.

* * *

The summer prior to meeting O'Brien, Mary went home to care for her mother, who had recently been diagnosed with cancer. During her visit, Mary's fans George and

Betty Stinson hosted her trio in their huge home in Sewickley, an affluent Pittsburgh suburb that was home to the Mellons and other famous families. Besides playing pieces that she would later use in her history of jazz concerts such as "Fandangle" and "My Mama Pinned a Rose on Me," Mary shared a new idea, speaking of her wish to mount a jazz benefit for Bel Canto in Pittsburgh. She had already mingled with Sewickley socialites at numerous events and knew that she was in the right place to seek financial backing from wealthy executives: George Stinson was the president of the National Steel Corporation and his wife, Betty (Millsop), was the daughter of the president of Weirton Steel. Both soon became key backers of Mary's new concert idea. Mary also knew that Pittsburgh was in the midst of an uptick in jazz support via Gateway Recordings, a new label that was recording local musicians, and Gulf Oil, a major sponsor of jazz workshops. Soon the city was receiving national attention in *DownBeat* via Roy Kohler, the magazine's new Pittsburgh jazz correspondent. The time was right for a large-scale jazz event.

In a spirit of bringing the church and the public together, Mary now sought backing for her benefit performance from the local Catholic diocese. After being introduced by Fr. Woods, she had been corresponding with the city's bishop, John J. Wright, for three years. In a letter addressed to Mary in early May 1963, Bishop Wright expressed regret at not being able to meet with Mary personally, as he was about to leave for Rome to attend the second session of Vatican II. Mary had written to Wright about the positive effects of jazz on young people and may have suggested a way to bring jazz and charitable work together with the church's assistance. But Wright had initially replied with the lament that music was "way out of his field and I cannot even advise."[11]

Mary's push for a Pittsburgh jazz event dovetailed not only with the Second Vatican Council but also with an overhaul of the local Catholic Youth Organization (CYO). Just one day prior to the opening session of Vatican II, Fr. Michael P. Williams became the new CYO director and was tasked with bringing more youth centers to urban neighborhoods. The CYO had one interracial youth center in the Hill District, the African American neighborhood that had suffered an insurmountable loss six years earlier when the city bulldozed a large section of the community to erect the Civic Arena, displacing more than 8,000 Hill residents in the process. An active, on-the-ground organizer who got things done, Fr. Williams told Mary that her Bel Canto Foundation was "terrific"[12] and soon played a large role in helping her produce her first jazz Mass for students at the all-girls Elizabeth Seton High School, where he served as chaplain.

Bishop Wright's earlier letter to Mary had been composed one month prior to the death of Pope John XXIII. The pope had surprised many four years earlier by announcing his intention to call the Second Vatican Council, the first convening of all the Catholic bishops across the world since 1869. Over the course of four two-month meetings from 1962 to 1965, Vatican II gathered more than 2,000 bishops and drafted four "constitutions," binding documents for local parishes that effected major changes in daily church life. When Bishop Wright's close friend Pope Paul VI succeeded Pope John XXIII, Wright became a key figure in the second conciliar meeting. The first document to come out of Vatican II, and the one that would affect Mary's sacred music the most, the Constitution on the Sacred Liturgy, was issued on December 4, 1963. The CSL emphasized the "full, active participation of the congregation"[13] and allowed Masses to be celebrated in the native language of the assembly. While these imperatives were intended to reform liturgy, the focus on using music reflective of local culture may have influenced Bishop Wright's decision to take Mary up on her jazz concert idea.

Whether because of the influence of Vatican II, Fr. Williams, or Mary's persistence, in early 1964 Bishop Wright gave the go-ahead for a local jazz festival. In *The Pittsburgh Press*, Wright commented that "by her own example [Mary had] convinced him and the Pittsburgh CYO that more knowledge about the cultural aspects of jazz can have beneficial spiritual results on young people."[14] However, rather than benefit Bel Canto as Mary had hoped, all concert proceeds would go toward the diocesan Catholic Youth Organization. As Mary had always worked to bring jazz to young people, she accepted the change in beneficiary and threw herself into the detailed work of organizing a festival. Mary connected Fr. Williams with Newport Jazz Festival director George Wein, contracting him as co-producer. Fr. Williams arranged for publicity, housing for artists, and all of the necessary budgeting, staying in touch with Mary through letters. To feature her sacred music, Mary reunited with Melba Liston for assistance with forming a festival big band comprised of New York and Pittsburgh musicians to perform new arrangements of "Saint Martin" and "Praise the Lord."

On April 9, 1964, Mary attended a press conference with Liston, Williams, Wright, and Wein where the first Pittsburgh Jazz Festival was formally announced for June 19 and 20 at the Civic Arena. Mary's Sewickley friends, the Stinsons—who were later listed in the event program among the festival's founders—were also in attendance. The array of scheduled talent included Thelonious Monk, vocalist Joe Williams, Dave Brubeck, and Ben Webster as well as musicians with Pittsburgh ties including Dakota Staton, Harold Betters, Walt

Harper, and Mary herself. Local press, especially the influential Black newspaper the *Pittsburgh Courier*, ran features leading up to the festival. *Courier* readers were keenly aware of the controversy that had surrounded the building of the Civic Arena. Many of the Hill's cultural and religious institutions, including Bethel African Methodist Episcopal Church and the Crawford Grill, the vibrant jazz club that had hosted many of the musicians on the jazz festival roster, had been demolished to make way for the arena. But Pittsburghers were—and remain today—rightfully proud of their jazz legacy and arrived in the thousands to show their support. Mary was the star of the two-day event, which opened and closed with the Pittsburgh Jazz Festival Orchestra, a big band comprised of Pittsburgh and New York players including trumpeters Eugene Edward "Snooky" Young and Thad Jones. In a unique marriage of liturgical dance and jazz, the Bernice Johnson Dancers, a troupe comprised of African American teenage dancers, performed to Liston's new arrangement of "Saint Martin" with the Pittsburgh Jazz Festival Orchestra, Mary at the piano, and vocalist Ethel Fields. Fans stayed for more than four and a half hours on the first night to hear jazz legends including Mary, Monk, Art Blakey, and trombonist Al Grey. Quoted in the *Courier* the next morning, Wein declared, "Jazz is fighting for respectability and acceptance and we have never had a grander opportunity than the one which the Catholic Church provided here. The artists knew this was one of the most important programs in which jazz has ever been involved and did not let them down."[15] In a glowing review in the *Saturday Review*, critic Stanley Dance underscored the festival's importance, writing, "What gives a jazz festival significance . . . is the new work it presents or inspires. In this respect, the chief architect was Mary Lou Williams, who happens to be an ardent Catholic and also one of the three outstanding pianists Pittsburgh has given to jazz."[16] Both Bishop Wright and Fr. Williams were impressed by the festival's artistic success, and Fr. Williams remarked that "most of those who listened to jazz for the first time were amazed at how exciting it is."[17] Bishop Wright commented that the event had "brought a little more beauty into the lives of thousands"[18] and pledged to present another edition in 1965.

Despite its musical success, the festival did not net a profit for the CYO. Mary wrote to Fr. Norman Weyand, SJ, the priest who had recently heard her perform at the Hickory House, expressing her disappointment at the festival's lack of financial success. In a reply dated July 15, Fr. Weyand asked that Mary take Fr. Woods's advice and consider "dropping the Bel Canto Foundation," reminding her that without governmental backing she could not "carry on both her work of music and personal charity the way that Dorothy Day or Baroness [Catherine] de Hueck," the founder of the Madonna House in Harlem, had done.[19]

Fr. Weyand wrote his letter one day before Mary's Harlem neighborhood was engulfed in a six-day riot, the second she had experienced since moving to New York twenty years earlier. The riots were set off after a New York policeman, Lieutenant Thomas Gilligan, shot and killed James Powell, a fifteen-year-old African American teenager, in front of his friends. In a second letter, Weyand consoled Mary with the reminder that "neither of us is responsible for all the injustice in the world," something that Mary needed to hear from a priest. Weyand praised the good that Mary had done in Pittsburgh, writing, "Your disappointing Pittsburgh festival, I understand, got good notices in *DownBeat*, the *Saturday Review*, and other periodicals. . . . charge the whole affair up 2 'profit & loss,' Mary Lou, and to the honor and glory of God. You did everything you could."[20]

Bishop Wright stayed true to his word and approved a second edition of the festival for 1965. The most historic concert to come out of that year's festival was a workshop that featured a microcosm of jazz piano history on one stage: stride pianist Willie "The Lion" Smith, Duke Ellington, Billy Taylor, Mary's early idol Earl "Fatha" Hines, Mary herself, and young pianist Charles Bell. The pianists performed in solo, duo, and trio combinations and answered questions in front of a live audience at Pittsburgh's Webster Hall. In the liner notes to *The Jazz Piano*, the live recording of the glorious event, Billy Taylor wrote, "In a field where it is considered a compliment to tell a woman she plays like a man, many men consider it a compliment to be told that they play like Mary Lou Williams."[21]

While Mary was not directly involved with the festival in its subsequent 1966, 1968, and 1970 editions, her presence was strongly felt. For the 1970 edition, local pianist Walt Harper replaced Wein as producer and was joined by Rev. John Ayoob, another priest fan of Mary's, as associate director. An amateur jazz pianist, Ayoob had followed Mary's 1964 comeback press and met Br. Mario while a seminarian at the North American College in Rome. Hearing Ayoob play at a student body event, Mario had shared Mary's *Black Christ of the Andes* recording and encouraged him to write to Mary. In an undated later (probably from 1964), Ayoob wrote, "I've been playing your album . . . and everybody here is really digging it. . . . You've been a tremendous inspiration to me and shown me more than ever before how intimately the two—jazz and religion—are related. Maybe I already knew this fact, but now the Church and Jazz has someone who is proving the validity of this thing to a wide audience."[22]

Mary was widening the circles of church, jazz, and community. Although the Pittsburgh Jazz Festival as sponsored by the CYO ended in 1970, the city has had various incarnations of a jazz festival in the decades since and currently hosts the annual Pittsburgh International Jazz Festival honoring a Pittsburgh jazz musician each year. Whether or not she is recognized as such, Mary is the pioneer who got the whole thing started.

CHAPTER EIGHT

Eternal and Everyday (1967–69)

> Now when I play, I feel it's a sort of prayer. Jazz arises from a spirit of love, it comes from the mind and heart and goes through the fingertips.
>
> —Mary Lou Williams, quoted in "Jazz Is Really Spiritual Music," *Pittsburgh Catholic* (February 23, 1973)

Although Mary had made forays into religious jazz in live performance and on record, she had not yet written jazz specifically to be used in the liturgy. Since her conversion in 1957, priests including Fr. Crowley, Fr. Norman O'Connor, and Fr. Woods had encouraged her to compose a new Mass setting. But on October 15, 1965, Fr. Woods, Mary's closest spiritual companion and the person who had pushed her back to her music the most, died from a heart attack. In Pittsburgh at the time of his death, Mary rushed back to New York to attend his requiem Mass at St. Francis Xavier Church. A friend described Mary's reaction to seeing Woods's body: "Mary and Lorraine [Gillespie] were so upset. Outside the chapel, Mary said, 'Why did they have to bury him with shoes with holes in them?' Mary was usually stoic, but she was crying. . . . We were all sad, but Mary was heartbroken."[1] Mary wrote of her loss to her priest and religious friends, including Fr. Weyand, who had just seen her at the 1965 Pittsburgh Jazz Festival. Urging her to keep going with her music, Weyand responded, "Father Woods was right: 'You must write the Jazz Mass. . . . Do it for Father Woods—he will help you—and dedicate it to him. If I can be of assistance in any way, you know that . . . I'll adopt you to the extent of my ability.' "[2]

Br. Mario joined in the chorus of friends encouraging Mary to compose. Writing eight months after Fr. Woods's death, he asked Mary, "Are you still doing your writing? I guess not now that you don't have Fr. Woods to press you on to write. You should write. God has given you this gift, try to put it to use."[3] Two weeks later, Mary replied that while she had written four new tunes, she "thought it best to drop the Mass—everybody has written a jazz Mass."[4]

It appears that Mary had contemplated the idea of writing a jazz Mass at least two years earlier: in her 1964 *Time* magazine feature, it was reported that she was working on a jazz Mass.[5] Now in 1966, Mary's reticence to write a jazz setting of the liturgy came at a time when religious music albums—including religious jazz—were constantly in the spotlight. Labels released folk musician Ray Repp's *Mass for Young Americans* and signed choirs of women religious congregations such as the Singing Sisters of Mount St. Mary with Mitch Miller, the popular television sing-along host. The surge in religious albums only intensified after "Dominique," a catchy song about St. Dominic recorded by a young Belgian novice known only as Soeur Sourire ("Sister Smile"), rose to the top of the pop charts in December of 1963. While Mary had independently released her 1964 religious jazz album *Black Christ of the Andes*, major record labels were releasing jazz Masses and sacred jazz concerts. In 1965 RCA Victor released flutist Paul Horn's *Jazz Suite on the Mass Texts*, a work composed by Lalo Schifrin with liner notes by Fr. Norman O'Connor, the Paulist "jazz priest" who had urged Mary to write a jazz Mass as early as 1957. The same year Fantasy Records released *Vince Guaraldi at Grace Cathedral*, a live recording of the pianist's jazz Mass in San Francisco. In 1966, two major religious jazz albums were released: Duke Ellington's *First Sacred Concert* on RCA Victor and pianist Joe Masters's *The Jazz Mass* on Columbia, the latter again with liner notes penned by Fr. O'Connor.

In other media, films in the mid-1960s also fueled a popular obsession with all things Catholic through a profusion of movies about nuns such as the 1966 film *The Singing Nun*, which was loosely based on Soeur Sourire.[6] Newspapers that had run daily reports on Vatican II soon incited a controversy over jazz Masses, which had flowered in this short period just after the Second Vatican Council and before the US Bishops' Conference on the Liturgy published definitive documents such as the Place of Music in Eucharistic Celebrations in 1968. On January 4, 1967, the Vatican's Congregation of Rites and the Commission for the Application of Vatican Council II's Constitution on the Sacred Liturgy issued a document stating that private home celebrations as well as "Masses offered using strange and arbitrary rites, vestments and formulas, and sometimes accompanied by music of a totally profane and worldly character, not worthy of a sacred action" were "not in conformity with the letter and spirit of the liturgical constitution of the Second Vatican Council."[7] The document was meant as a response to "family Eucharistic banquets"—Masses that lay people were conducting in their homes—which the council initially saw as a misinterpretation of the *aggiornamento* (modernization) that they were seeking to encourage.

The day after the national *Catholic News Service* released the English translation of the document, newspapers reacted with headlines such as "Jazz Mass Included in Ban by Vatican on 'Strange' Rites,"[8] incorrectly reporting the directive as a papal ban on jazz Masses. But as Fr. Clement J. McNaspy, SJ, pointed out two weeks later in the Jesuit magazine *America*, nowhere in the document was there any reference to jazz. McNaspy chided the papers for "irresponsible editorializing" and commented that if Europe had recently celebrated Masses with unsuitable music, America's "greater liturgical peril is not too much zest but too much ennui."[9]

Amid the controversy, Mary received her first liturgical jazz commission from Fr. McNaspy as part of an ecumenical concert at Carnegie Hall sponsored by the New York Jesuits. Partnering with Avant Garde Records, a small label focused on folk and religious music, the Jesuits commissioned six composers to write new religious works for a performance entitled *Praise the Lord in Many Voices*. The artists included folk-rock musician John Ylvisaker and Sr. Miriam Therese Winter with the Medical Mission Sisters, both on the Avant Garde roster; symphonic composer Fr. Bruno Markaitis, SJ; folk artist and Jesuit seminarian Paul Quinlan; and New York Philharmonic composer-in-residence David Amram.

Composing three new choral pieces for the Carnegie premiere, Mary juggled her writing with volunteer work with children at a community center on 112th Street and with the opening of her new Harlem clothing shop, Votre Boutique. A glance at the *New York Amsterdam News* shows Mary's prominence in Harlem as well as her extremely busy schedule: in the January 28, 1967, edition, an ad for the boutique lists an open house running from January 31 through February 4;[10] on page seven of the February 4 edition, Mary and several models are pictured at the shop's champagne opening with Hazel Scott, recently returned from Paris, as the guest of honor.[11] Mary again appears in a concert preview on page sixteen and her name is prominently displayed two pages later in a concert advertisement.[12]

On February 5, the day after the *Amsterdam News* preview, Mary performed in the historic concert that was recorded and released as a three LP set on Avant Garde. During her twenty-minute segment, Fr. McNaspy narrated Mary's story using text that clearly came from Mary herself. In a condensed "history of jazz" that would soon become a standard part of Mary's concert programs, McNaspy briefly outlined the eras of jazz as defined by Mary: spirituals, ragtime, Kansas City swing, and boogie-woogie, with Mary providing short solo piano demonstrations of each. For the final era that Mary called "modern" music, she was joined by bassist Bill Salter and drummer Percy Brice on "Joycie," an original funk tune that she had recorded at the 1965 Pittsburgh Jazz Festival piano workshop.

Mary's three newly commissioned choral works, as arranged by Melba Liston, provided the evening's highlights. A twenty-five-voice "interfaith choir" joined Mary's trio with guest vocalist Leon Thomas on the blues-drenched "Thank You, Jesus," with lyrics that paraphrased portions of Psalm 37. "Our Father," with its gorgeous *a cappella* choral introduction, followed by Honi Gordon's solo verses accented with lush choral backgrounds, was the most moving piece of the program. Mary would use adaptations of this same version of the "Our Father" in all three of her subsequent Masses. She ended her set with Thomas in a preacher-like role as he called out short riffs followed by jubilant choral responses on "Praise the Lord (Come,

Holy Spirit)," the work that had closed her *Black Christ of the Andes* album.

In a review that appeared several weeks later, Fr. McNaspy singled out both Mary's and David Amram's contributions as "eternal," as opposed to "everyday," writing:

> Most of the program was easy to take on first hearing . . . and unlikely to change the history of music, or even to be ultimately reckoned "eternal." Exceptions were surely Mary Lou Williams' three new jazz spirituals . . . and David Amram's immensely moving *Shir L'erev Shabbat* (Sabbath Eve service). Both composers said something in private that I feel should be shared. Almost tearfully, Miss Williams asked whether her "Our Father" would ever be used in church; I replied that I certainly hoped so, and expected that we would both live to see the day. Mr. Amram's remark was that now his great ambition was to write a Catholic Mass, and hoped he might receive such a commission.[13]

But while the more mainstream artists—Sr. Miriam Therese Winter, John Ylvsaker, and Paul Quinlan—all had their new works not only recorded but published by the World Library of Sacred Music (the precursor to World Library Publications), Mary was still on her own in figuring out how to get her sacred music into more widespread use.

Mary now expressed interest in composing a Mass, and wrote to Moe Asch at Folkways Records to see if he would consider producing such a work. Noticing the popular appeal that artists like the Medical Mission Sisters were enjoying, Mary wrote, "The Catholic priests and nuns are making a lot of money on records now."[14] Even though Asch declined her request, Mary soon received a built-in opportunity to compose a Mass. For three years, she had corresponded with

Fr. Michael Williams, who had continued to promote her music among Pittsburgh youth at Catholic Youth Organization dances. In a letter to Mary in October 1966, Fr. Williams noted the teenagers' enthusiastic response: "The youth of Pittsburgh are Mary Lou-happy. . . . Everywhere we go kids are talking about you."[15] Seeking a way for Mary to work directly with young people, Fr. Williams secured a position for her at Elizabeth Seton High School, the all-girls school run by the Sisters of Charity in Pittsburgh's Brookline neighborhood where he served as chaplain. In the spring of 1967, Mary began teaching a class of twenty-five at Seton, experimenting until she figured out how to connect with the girls. In her words, "I was teaching them theory and the kids just sat there and glared at me. I couldn't stand that, so finally I said, 'Let's do it how it is.' I wrote a bop blues and the kids went wild."[16] Realizing that she was in a perfect position to both engage the students and hear her music sung as she created it, Mary began writing her first Mass setting, teaching the girls eight measures at a time. In a letter to Peter O'Brien, the young Jesuit seminarian who would soon begin working as Mary's manager, Mary enthused, "Can't seem to write in New York, but listen to this. There's eight of us where I live [at her sister Mamie's house] . . . kids are running up and down the stairs, TV on in the room to the left and to the right. . . . Yet I stay up at 4 AM frequently, writing for the kids—something else, huh?"[17]

With a choir of thirteen girls from Seton, Mary's first Mass was premiered at St. Paul Cathedral, the mother church of the Pittsburgh diocese, located directly across the street from where she had played at the 1965 jazz piano workshop at Webster Hall. On Wednesday morning, July 26, 1967, Mary's *Pittsburgh Mass* was sung in a public liturgy sponsored by the CYO's Summer School of

Christian Apostolate with Bishop Wright celebrating. In a *Pittsburgh Catholic* preview, Mary explained that she tried to capture in the Mass "the way I feel when I'm praying."[18] All of the movements were sung by the girls in unison with Mary at the piano. Two of the work's highlights are the "Gloria," with its unexpected harmonies and tempo changes that reflect the various sections of the lengthy text, and the "Our Father." Mary would simplify the "Our Father" in her third and most well-known Mass, *Music for Peace*, but her more embellished 1967 version, both as sung at St. Paul and at Carnegie Hall, reflects a depth of prayer conveyed through breathtaking melodic lines that leave the listener with a deep sense of awe.

It appears that the *Pittsburgh Mass* was performed only on one more occasion, during the following summer. It is only because Mary had the foresight to record a rehearsal on her cassette player that we have any recorded evidence of the work today. Both Mary's scores and the recording are housed in her archival collection at the Institute of Jazz Studies at Rutgers University.

* * *

Mary continued to travel between Pittsburgh and New York for the next several months and briefly taught again at Seton in the fall. With mounting financial worries exacerbated by several break-ins to her apartment, Mary returned to composing big band music, something she hadn't done since leaving the Clouds fifteen years earlier. She hounded Duke Ellington, letting him know that she was available to write for his orchestra. While Ellington's response remains unclear, Mary went ahead and composed five new works, sending them to Ellington to perform. A standout is "Truth," a major revision of her 1940 composition "Scratchin' in the Gravel," in an ultra-slow tempo updated with modern, rich harmony. Though Ellington never performed any of these pieces, Mary played them the following year with the Danish Radio Jazz Orchestra.

Mary's financial worries were compounded by health issues. Writing to Br. Mario, she listed her troubles, numbering each. She began, "I've been sitting in the house since 8/25/67 writing for Duke Ellington and it doesn't seem I'm getting any loot for it. He's begged me since 1941 to write for him—that is, pleaded. 2. I have kidney & bladder ailment. 3. During the course of writing I left the house to go to the P.O. [probably to send Ellington the new pieces] & someone broke in & robbed me of TV, new typewriter, the only good piece of luggage I had . . ."[19] Mary also mentioned her concern for her nephew Robbie, whom she had been trying to help by asking various priests to assist him in applying to boarding schools. But Mary confided in Br. Mario that Robbie "hasn't got a chance" and expressed her own exhaustion, describing herself as "old and haggard."[20]

Several months later, Mary's spirits were lifted on receiving a letter from Fr. Robert Ledogar, a Maryknoll priest who was a new appointee to the Music Advisory Board of the US Bishops' Commission on the Liturgical Apostolate. Working with a group of Harlem Catholic parishes to commission a series of seasonal Masses by local African American composers, Ledogar approached Mary about writing a Mass setting for Lent. The Masses were to be part of a series of "experiments in Sunday worship of a more contemporary style"[21] to take place at St. Thomas the Apostle Church on West 118th Street. Working with St. Thomas's pastor, Fr. Kevin Kelly, Fr. Ledogar had already contacted two additional composers: Billy Taylor, Mary's longtime friend since the 1950s, and Eddie Bonnemère, who had studied with Mary in the 1940s. In addition to his work as a public school music teacher, Bonnemère was the choir director at St. Thomas and had premiered his own jazz liturgy, *Missa Hodierna*, the previous year at Harlem's St. Charles Borromeo Church. Ledogar invited Bonnemère to compose an Advent Mass and to serve as music director for the project.

Excited by the prospect of writing a new Mass to be sung for all six Sundays of Lent, Mary readily agreed to write the second Mass in the series. After meeting in person, Fr. Ledogar sent Scripture text for Mary to consider as a starting point, writing, "I hope you take them as ideas to work with, not as something that can't be changed. . . . The most important thing is to have parts that the people can all sing, that can be taught to them in a few minutes without their having to read music."[22] Ledogar contributed his own text to the "Kyrie," adding, "For our lack of hope/ for our failure to care/for letting ourselves be paralyzed with fear . . ."[23] Mary wrote an easy-to-teach setting, with the youth choir singing the new text and the assembly joining in on "Lord, have mercy."

To augment St. Thomas's youth choir, Mary recruited children from the community center where she taught during the week. In Pittsburgh, Fr. Williams arranged for six of the Seton high schoolers to travel to New York to sing at the premiere (due to weather, the students were unable to make the trip). Mary also formed an instrumental sextet including saxophone, flute, guitar, bass, and drums with herself at the organ. Honi Gordon, the vocalist who had sung Mary's "Our Father" at the Carnegie Hall concert, led the congregation as cantor.

In an effort to record her Lenten Mass, Mary reached out to Moe Asch, asking if he would bring a crew to record one of the Sunday services for release on Folkways. Although Asch did record one of the liturgies, nothing further was done with the tape, probably due to poor sound quality. But for all of her unsuccessful efforts to have this major work recorded, Mary missed out on an opportunity right under her nose. Six weeks before the premiere, Ledogar informed Mary that he had received a call from Omer Westendorf, the president of the World Library of Sacred Music. Westendorf wanted to record and publish Mary's new work so that other assemblies could use the sheet music. In a January 16, 1968, letter postscript to Ledogar, Westendorf wrote, "It is growing very late to promote . . . a Lenten Mass for this coming Lent. If Mary Lou Williams would get the music to us soon, perhaps we can still get it in production and advertise it."[24] There is no record of Mary having provided a score to Ledogar or Westendorf, and like the *Pittsburgh Mass*, the only available recording of *Mass for the Lenten Season* is housed at the Institute of Jazz Studies at Rutgers University.

On March 3, 1968, *Mass for the Lenten Season* premiered at St. Thomas the Apostle with Mary at the organ and Bonnemère conducting. As evidenced on a homemade recording, the Psalm 27 setting of "The Lord is my light and my helper / of whom shall I be afraid?" comforts and encourages in a melody that stays in one's ear and the "Kyrie" with Ledogar's new text enlivens the assembly cries for God's mercy. Perhaps most dramatically, Mary's use of solo voice and acoustic bass on the "Anamnesis" ("dying, you destroyed our death / rising, you restored our life") with the entire assembly joining in singing the final phrase ("we will sing of you to all the world") feels like a resurrection in body, spirit, and community.

One of the congregants who sang Mary's new Mass was Dorothy Day, founder of the Catholic Worker. Day and Mary had been introduced via Janet Burwash, a former volunteer at Mary's first thrift shop. Day wrote of her experience attending Mass on the third Sunday of Lent:

> I have just come from a glorious celebration, the eleven o'clock Mass at St. Thomas the Apostle Church. . . . One came away feeling as though one had truly celebrated Mass, offering worship, adoration, glory to God, not to speak of penitence. . . . There is a climax of beauty at the singing of the choir, after the Sanctus. . . . As for the Great Amen, which is still more or less ignored in all our local churches, it is hard to describe the ecstatic "Glory to God, to Jesus Christ," and the half dozen repeated Amens followed by a final strong one sung by the entire congregation. This was a musical event; and I do not think there has been anything to compare with it in any of the so-called folk masses being sung in colleges and churches around the country.[25]

Mary wrote to Day expressing her gratitude: "Thank you very much for coming to the Mass—was quite surprised. . . . You inspired everyone."[26] In the same letter and in several to follow, Mary mentioned her financial strain. It appears that Day was trying to help Mary apply for a grant. Mary wrote, "Rev. Gensel [pastor of the jazz community at Saint Peter's Church], Fr. Ledogar and Billy Taylor are supposed to . . . talk about putting on a benefit for me to raise over $1500 to pay my bills. You know Dorothy it's difficult to do things I'm trying to do when there's no salary etc coming in—and I have been very fortunate. Fr. Kelly at St. Thomas and Bishop Wright in Pgh, Penna are the only ones that are salaried minded."[27]

Three nights before Mary's final liturgy on Palm Sunday, every television and radio in the country broadcast the shocking news that Martin Luther King Jr. had been assassinated. Day wrote in the *Catholic Worker* of her experience on receiving the news, describing how music—and Mary's in particular—had helped her: "Always, I think, I will weep when I hear the song, 'We Shall Overcome,' and when I read the words, 'Free at last, great God, free at last.' But the healing of grief is in those words that I had been hearing sung every Sunday at the Church of the St. Thomas the Apostle, in the Mass composed by Mary Lou Williams, herself a Black composer and jazz musician, herself internationally famous. 'I am the resurrection and the life. He who believes in me shall never die but have life everlasting.' "[28]

Mary responded immediately to Dr. King's death by writing two pieces that she taught to the St. Thomas youth choir. "Tell Him Not to Talk Too Long" sets a portion of King's February 4, 1968, sermon at Ebenezer Baptist Church in Mary's birthplace of Atlanta. Mary only slightly paraphrases King's original speech in the first verse: "If you're around when I meet my day / don't want a long funeral / and if somebody delivers the eulogy / tell him not to talk too long. Just say I tried to feed the hungry / tried to love somebody / If you're around when I meet my day / tell him not to talk too long."[29] The blues-inflected song contrasts with the jazz waltz feel of "I Have a Dream," based on a portion of King's famous speech from the 1963 March on Washington. Day invited Mary to share her musical tribute the following July at the annual Pax conference held at the Catholic Worker Farm in Tivoli, New York.

Two days after Easter Sunday, Mary wrote to Day from Pittsburgh, saying that she was taking "a breathing spell."[30] But Mary never rested for long. She now expressed her desire to do a concert for the pope. She had been trying to find a way to get her Lenten Mass performed in Rome, writing to Br. Mario and other religious for assistance. While Br. Mario assured her that he could get the North American

College seminarians to sing the Mass, he explained that an audience with the pope would probably be impossible. But with her typical determination, Mary worked on lining up gigs in Copenhagen, figuring that if she could get herself to Denmark it would be only a short matter of time before she could travel to Rome and have her Mass performed there. Fr. McNaspy had already recommended that Mary's portion of the 1967 Carnegie Hall concert be aired on Vatican Radio, and Mary was sure that other opportunities would follow.

Mary's tenacity paid off: she received an offer to play at a new club in Copenhagen and planned to leave for Europe in early May 1968. But the day before her departure, her sister Grace attempted suicide. Mary delayed her trip, staying in Pittsburgh before playing at the Catholic Worker's July conference in Tivoli. Two weeks later, she boarded a German steamer for her second trip to Europe, one that would lead her to Rome and to a commission to write her third and most well-known Mass, *Music for Peace*.

CHAPTER NINE

A Musical Contemplative
(1968–74)

> The saint and the artist do not belong to different realms. . . . They are wide open to their own experience far more profoundly than the rest of us. . . . I suggest we form our own litany of artists . . . Armstrong, Ellington, Coltrane, Monk, Gillespie and Mary Lou Williams.
>
> —Fr. Peter O'Brien, SJ, quoted in Jane Allison, "Bach Moves Over for Mary Lou at St. Pat's," *Indianapolis News* (February 22, 1975)

Armed with scores for her Lenten Mass and her new big band compositions, in August of 1968, Mary boarded a steamer to Denmark. She was still afraid to fly, but the five-day journey gave her time to reflect on her purpose in making her second trip to Europe, her first in sixteen years. This time, she was not traveling to headline a concert tour: instead, she was scheduled to perform a low-paying, five-nights-a-week, five-sets-per-night gig at Baron Timme Rosenkrantz's new Copenhagen club. Mary would have never accepted such a gig in the States, but she had a larger purpose: to get to Rome, where she hoped to gain a private audience with Pope Paul VI and have her Lenten Mass performed at the Vatican. While her plans did not materialize in the exact manner that she wished, Mary was aware that she would need to set time apart for spiritual rejuvenation. Mary had struggled throughout her career to reconcile her desire to "retreat" from the world versus her pull to perform. Her many letters to women religious show that she made religious retreats throughout the 1960s and 1970s. Even her letters to Br. Mario written from Copenhagen explained that when she arrived in Rome, she wanted to go on retreat to prepare for the work ahead. Little did she know that what would become a five-month stay in Denmark would include an extended retreat that would introduce her to another active contemplative who had been inspired by her music.

* * *

Arriving in Copenhagen, Mary found that Timmes Club was far from ready to open. Owner Timme Rosenkrantz found her a room, where she waited until October to begin her nightly appearances. Known as "the jazz baron," Rosenkrantz came from Danish nobility and was the host of a jazz program on Danish National Radio (now Radio Denmark). He had arranged for Mary to perform on two broadcasts with the Danish Radio Jazz Orchestra (still vital today as the DR Radio Big Band), providing her an opportunity to have the five arrangements she had written for Ellington to finally be performed. Mary took advantage of the delay in her club engagement by writing a new big band piece, "Aries Mood," to include on the program, and dedicated the work to her old friend, saxophonist Ben Webster.

She alternated these big band pieces with two of her favorite trio arrangements of Walter Donaldson's "My Blue Heaven" and Billy Taylor's "It's a Grand Night for Swinging." None of Mary's big band works from 1967 to 1968 were commercially recorded until more than forty-five years later when the Dutch Jazz Orchestra based in the Netherlands recorded the magnificent *Rediscovered Music of Mary Lou Williams: The Lady Who Swings the Band*.[1]

Beginning her engagement at Timmes Club in October, Mary moved into artist housing attached to the venue. In a letter to Dorothy Day, she described her grueling schedule: "Well, I'm still slaving for the glory of God. Hours from 9 PM 'til 2 AM—last week 9 PM till 4 AM playing 45 minute sets off 15 & 20 minutes, back on again."[2] Mary also mentioned her financial troubles, saying that she was paying off $2,000 worth of debt. But she was just as stressed from her working environment: Inez Cavanaugh, Rosenkrantz's girlfriend, constantly yelled at the servers, making the small room uncomfortably tense. In one of many desperate-sounding letters that she wrote with alarming frequency to Br. Mario, Mary said she "was almost 'nuts' " before Dizzy and Lorraine Gillespie came for a visit.[3] Becoming offended when Br. Mario did not reply as swiftly as she would have liked, Mary filled her letters with reprimands for his silence as well as insistent suggestions that he set up concerts on her behalf. But months earlier, Br. Mario had told Mary that he had planned to visit the States and would not be returning to Rome until late October. He had repeatedly requested that Mary inform him of her arrival date in Rome, as he wanted to set up a concert at the North American College where he had already shared her music with his fellow seminarians. But Mary had no definite plans and simply kept on asking Br. Mario when she should arrive, chiding him for not writing her back.

Mary now had a more pressing problem than setting up dates in Rome: she had to give up her artist housing to pianist Teddy Wilson, who had recently arrived to follow her as the featured performer at Timmes Club. A solution came out of Mary's prayer practice: while attending daily Mass, she asked a woman who sat in front of the sacraments to pray for her. She credited those prayers with guiding her to a local priest who asked the sisters at a Benedictine convent if they might have an available guest room. The sisters replied that they did, and on November 10, 1968, Mary moved into the St. Lioba Cloister in the center of Copenhagen. With this move, the tone of her letters shifted from desperation to contentment. With time off from the club, Mary took a spiritual retreat. In a letter to Br. Mario, she described the joy she experienced in the cloister, writing, "After I moved here with the NUNS I broke down & laughed so loud if anyone heard me, they probably thought I was nuts!" One of the sisters brought her a copy of *The Sign of Jonas*, a collection of Thomas Merton's journal entries from his first five years as a Trappist monk. Mary wrote that she "[could not] get enough of it" and included a passage from the book where Merton quotes St. John of the Cross: "In order to arrive at knowing all / Desire to know nothing in anything / In order to arrive at being all / Desire to be nothing in anything."[4] Mary also said that reading Merton "cooled" her, a term she often used to describe when her soul felt at peace. Ironically, Merton was also a fan of Williams. On New Year's Eve of 1967, he recorded a "jazz meditation" in his hermitage in Kentucky where he listened and verbally responded to jazz albums by Williams and guitarist Wes Montgomery. Merton invited listeners to "participate in this New Year's Eve party of one or rather two, me and my girlfriend, Mary Lou Williams. But Mary Lou Williams is on a record. She is a Kansas City pianist and . . . it's the kind of music that strikes all kinds of responses in my own heart."[5] While Mary was traveling to Denmark, Merton was simultaneously heading to Asia to speak at an interfaith conference in Bangkok, Thailand, where he died in a bizarre accident. Mary had no knowledge of Merton prior to her European trip. In a January 4, 1969, letter to Br. Mario penned one month after Merton's death, Mary wrote, "Really something how I read his books a few weeks before he passed away. Couldn't believe he'd died until I received a letter from a friend in the USA—Ed Rice is a friend of mine—& I think I know most of his friends."[6] It is amazing that Mary and Merton never met, considering that both Ed Rice and Mary's friend Barry Ulanov had been Merton's close friends at Columbia University and all actively sought out live jazz. Yet even without a physical encounter, through meeting Merton in his journals, Mary had found another companion of the spirit.

Strengthened by her spiritual retreat, Mary now prepared to travel to Rome, where Br. Mario had formed a choir of seminarians ready to sing her *Mass for the Lenten Season*. As she boarded a train from Copenhagen, sent off by Timme Rosenkrantz and the Saint Lioba sisters, she was filled with anticipation at what the place she had dreamed of for so long would bring.

* * *

After arriving in Rome, Mary began to realize that she had been overly demanding in her letters to Br. Mario. Meeting the friar for dinner, she apologized for pushing for a salary to perform her Lenten Mass but also implied that she would have been more patient if she had been able to schedule a few days of quiet. Mary had no cause to worry, as Br. Mario had already laid the groundwork for her visit. He introduced her to the abbot general of the Benedictines, Fr. Rembert Weakland, OSB, a Juilliard-trained pianist who was one of the key players in the implementation of liturgical music reform after Vatican II. Fr. Weakland shared another connection with Mary: he was from Latrobe, Pennsylvania, just forty miles east of Pittsburgh. He was also a colleague of Fr. Bob Ledogar: both were on the Music Advisory Board, the committee that had drafted the *Place of Music in Eucharistic Celebrations* in 1968.

Weakland organized a tribute Mass for Martin Luther King Jr. to feature Mary performing her *Mass for the Lenten Season* at the Pontifical Latin American College. The event was publicized heavily, and more than fifty television and newspaper reporters came to cover the liturgy. But the evening before the service, Weakland informed Mary that she would have to perform the music as a post-Mass concert. The sudden change had occurred after a conversation between Weakland and Cardinal Angelo Dell'Acqua, vicar general for Rome. Dell'Acqua was opposed to the use of drums and canceled the jazz Mass. The irony is that Mary had planned to use bongos, a hand percussion instrument with much less sound than a standard drum kit, and was not asked if she would consider omitting the instrument for this particular liturgy.

Just prior to the Mass, Weakland announced to the assembly of mostly Americans that "unexpected interest from the scores of newsmen who filled the modern circular chapel . . . made it necessary to have the music played after the Mass was complete." He also said that it had been his decision to have the music performed separately "as an examination of conscience to know whether we have really come here to hear Mass or hear a jazz concert."[7] But anyone who had followed Weakland's work knew of his strong support for experimenting with different musical styles in the liturgy. The sudden change was a blow to Mary, though she shrugged off the press in her usual manner, replying to inquiries from reporters that she was not hurt by the decision. But she was. Several months later when Mary read an article saying that Cardinal Dell'Acqua was pro jazz Masses, she complained that "everything is jazz now—and everybody receives recognition 'cept us."[8]

Even with the last-minute setback, Mary's concert was an overwhelming success. Along with a student guitarist, bassist, and bongo player, Mary accompanied a choir of thirty seminarians from the colleges of North American, Propaganda Fide, and St. Anselm. Titled "Jazz for the Soul," the performance featured the full *Mass for the Lenten Season* as well as "Tell Him Not to Talk Too Long," Mary's Martin Luther King Jr. tribute. The following day newspapers worldwide reported on Mary's blues-informed setting of Dr. King's words as well as Weakland's reaction: "Weakland was smiling broadly and repeated several times, 'I am very pleased.' . . . When asked if he would consider doing the same thing in the future, he laughed and said: 'If we do, we won't let anybody know about it.' "[9] And Mary said, "I would have liked to play my music at the Mass but I understand the way it is."[10]

Two days later, Mary visited the Vatican in a semi-private audience with Pope Paul VI, who gave her a blessing and a rosary. Seizing her chance, Mary "blurted out that I'd like to do a concert for him. He almost blushed and smiled like a little boy, but nothing said."[11] While a concert for the pope never occurred, Mary performed twice on Vatican Radio, playing her two Martin Luther King Jr. tribute pieces with the North American seminarians in February, and giving a solo interview/performance in April just prior to leaving Rome.

Many priests continued to make crucial introductions for Mary. Seminarian Peter O'Brien had mentioned Mary's work to Fr. Vincent O'Keefe, SJ, an assistant to the general of the Jesuit Fathers. O'Keefe arranged a meeting between Mary and Msgr. Joseph Gremillion, a priest from Louisiana who was secretary of the new Pontifical Commission on Justice and Peace. The commission worked with aid organizations, including the World Bank and the Peace Corps, in promoting the development of third world nations and had recently created a new liturgy for a votive Mass for peace and justice. Not knowing the purpose of their meeting, Mary was shocked when Gremillion offered her a commission to compose a new musical setting using the new Mass texts. Mary immediately wrote to Fr. Bob Ledogar, asking if he would work with her on the new Mass. Although he was about to leave for Africa, Ledogar replied that he could put in a few evenings with her upon her return to New York. Gremillion gave Mary several Scripture snippets to be sung in the new Mass, and it appears that Mary also shared text and music with him, possibly her "Kyrie" from *Mass for the Lenten Season*. Mary described this exchange in a letter to Br. Mario that she wrote during her voyage home: "Msgr. Joseph Gremillion . . . said the text was accepted but the music would never be accepted . . . but I'll still continue to write. We have to reach the younger generation."[12] Without the requirement to tailor her composing for a specific parish or ensemble, Mary had the freedom to create a new Mass that would reach a larger target audience: the youth she loved so dearly.

* * *

Having received an official Vatican validation of her sacred music, Mary was now ready to go home after seven months in Europe. From aboard the *Michelangelo* steamer, she wrote Br. Mario five letters, half joking that she expected five in return. Complaining about her weight problems and commenting that she couldn't walk because her "heart gets tired & feet are swelling,"[13] Mary went to the hospital on board and stayed on a diet and exercise regimen for the five-day journey. She also expressed concern for Joe Glaser, her former agent. Glaser had recently written to Mary about a potential engagement at the posh Plaza Hotel in New York. Mary asked Br. Mario to "pray hard" both that she would get the gig and for Glaser's health, as he was quite ill (he died two months later). One of Mary's prayers was answered: she was offered the Plaza Hotel engagement, but after arriving home, she turned it down, deciding instead to focus her energies on the new Mass. Her desire to remove distractions, however, did not extend to her relatives. Mary's old friend Roland Mayfield drove her to Pittsburgh to celebrate her birthday, and soon after, drove both Mary's sister Mamie and her mother, Virginia, to New York. In her journal, Mary wrote of her family frustrations: "Mamie had to fool Mom to get her over here. Been on my knees cleaning for days. Mom wanted to leave. . . . Mom and her snuff and gin. I am old, fat, and tired." The following day she wrote, "Fought sister Grace, wanted to punch her in the mouth for throwing a lighted cigarette in Robert's face. . . . Please forgive me God for not being more charitable. Must get the weight off, am choking in the throat."[14]

After her family returned to Pittsburgh, Mary began working on the Mass in earnest. She had barely finished her first draft when she was contacted by Fr. Harold Salmon, SJ, the first Black priest to be appointed pastor in the Archdiocese of New York. The thirty-nine-year-old served as pastor of St. Charles Borromeo Church and head of the Harlem Vicariate, the group of seven Harlem parishes that had commissioned Mary to write her Lenten Mass the previous year. Now a tragic event led to a need for Mary's new Mass. Tom Mboya, the young Kenyan statesman who was expected to be the next president of his country, was assassinated on July 5, 1969, at the age of thirty-nine, the same age as Fr. Salmon. Salmon had been asked to celebrate Mboya's memorial at Holy Family Church on East 47th Street, with many United Nations delegates expected to be in attendance. Knowing the significance that Mary would bring as an African American, Catholic, woman, and jazz musician, he asked if she would perform her new Mass at the memorial.

Mary agreed to present her work in progress, even though she had very little time: the Mboya memorial was to be held in just over a week. She hired vocalist Leon Thomas to join her and added a bassist and flutist at the last minute. With the Mass's thematic focus on peace, Mary wrote a new song with both original music and text, "People in Trouble," as a prelude. The lyrics captured Mary's feelings after witnessing the 1968 riots that had erupted after Martin Luther King Jr.'s death, especially in Harlem and Pittsburgh's Hill District. The words now applied to the tension between the rival Luo and Kikuyu Kenyan tribes: "People in trouble, children in pain / too weak to care, too mean to share / worked so hard tryin' to find a brother / became impatient / now we hate each other." The song then asks for God's help and closes with, "You are the resurrection and the life. Save us before we perish."[15] For this first edition of her Mass, Mary did not include a setting of the Creed or a Gloria, instead focusing on the short Scripture passages that Gremillion had given her, including verses from Psalm 72 ("In his day / justice shall flourish / and peace / till the moon fails") and John 14:27 ("Peace I leave with you / my peace I give to you").

Following the Mboya memorial, Mary began to recast her Mass in a more jazz-rock mode with the goals of reaching young people and having the work be used in other countries. She wrote to Msgr. Gremillion, who promised to share the Mass with other associates but reminded Mary that language might prove a barrier to performing the work internationally. She also contacted Bob Banks, an arranger who had conducted the interfaith choir at the 1967 Carnegie Hall concert. Banks had experience in more popular music styles and Mary hoped that his input would help make her Mass more accessible to youth. Mary also wanted to record the Mass. As the funds from her commission were not large enough to cover studio costs, she approached Fr. Ed Flanagan, a Maryknoll priest who had recently made a short film on her work with young people. Fr. Flanagan contributed $6,000 toward production costs for the new album to be called *Music for Peace*. Running out of money after two sessions, Mary set the project aside, only continuing after the urging of Dizzy Gillespie and her half brother Jerry Burley.

In May of 1970, Mary released *Music for Peace* on her Mary Records imprint. A standout moment on the album features bassist-vocalist Carline Ray's vocal solo on "Lazarus" with a text contributed by guitarist Sonny Henry. For the "Creed," Mary set the shorter Apostles' Creed after having struggled in her first Mass with the lengthy Nicene Creed. David Amram, one of the composers from the 1967 Carnegie Hall concert, played French horn, improvising a part on Mary's new "Gloria" with text by Fr. Ledogar. Mary would return to the Credo and the Gloria on many occasions, performing both as instrumentals. She also included Leon Thomas's original "The World" as a communion song, explaining that it provided "a hopeful alternative" to "People in Trouble." Thomas's lyric begins, "If we all could love one another, then the world would be as one."[16] While the album was recorded piecemeal with two different sets of instrumentalists and vocalists, it nevertheless sounds coherent as a musical and liturgical statement.

A month after the release, Mary gave a live premiere of *Music for Peace* at St. Paul's Chapel at Columbia University to glowing reviews. She wrote letters to friends in high places who she hoped would promote the Mass and sent the album to Msgr. Gremillion, asking for $2,000 to help with publicity expenses. While he was unable to assist financially, Gremillion sent Mary a list of priests to send the record to along with a check to cover purchase and shipping costs. Writing letters and making trips to the post office were part of the day-to-day business of Mary's career, something she had always dealt with herself even when she had part-time managers. She now decided to ask for help to meet the demands that accompanied a groundswell of critical attention. Fr. Peter O'Brien had stayed in close contact with Mary since their meeting at the Hickory House six years earlier. After attending college in Maryland and on the West Coast, O'Brien had returned to New York. Mary now asked if he would be her manager. O'Brien recalled: "I remember it was in her Cadillac, parked on 102nd Street and Riverside Drive late at night, before I went upstairs to where I lived. Mary said: 'I'll go out if you come with me.' And I decided my ministry should be Mary Lou and saving jazz. I said yes."[17] Even while serving as an associate priest at St. Ignatius Loyola Church from 1972 to 1977, O'Brien worked as Mary's manager until her death in 1981.

Even with Fr. O'Brien's assistance, Mary still remained involved in the business side of her career. She had already written to Cardinal Terence Cooke suggesting the possibility of having a jazz Mass at St. Patrick's Cathedral, the seat of the New York archdiocese in midtown Manhattan. Attending O'Brien's ordination at Fordham University in 1971, Mary saw Cooke and seized the opportunity. As she described it, "Peter [O'Brien] hid behind a tree and I went chasing across the campus shouting, 'Cardinal Cooke! Cardinal Cooke!' I told him I'd written a Mass and I'd like to do it at Saint Patrick's. He said, 'fine.' I said, 'It's kind of noisy and loud.' 'That's what we need,' he said."[18]

It would take several years before Mary played her Mass at the cathedral. In the meantime she received new engagements that kept her in the public eye. One of the most long lasting came via a reunion with Barney Josephson, the entrepreneur who had done so much for her career in the 1940s at Café Society. Josephson had recently opened a restaurant in Greenwich Village called the Cookery. While visiting the eatery with Fr. O'Brien, Mary directly asked Josephson if he would get a piano for her to play in the restaurant. The two made a deal that Josephson would rent a piano of Mary's choosing for four months, during which time Mary would play nightly. And so it was that Mary found her new jazz home in New York, opening on November 20, 1970, and staying for several months each year through 1976. Press again heralded her "return to the jazz world" and Josephson bought the piano after Mary's first month. He later recalled what she had told him: "We did it, Barney. You and me and the Lord Jesus Christ."[19]

Through Fr. O'Brien's efforts, a new collaboration was about to begin between Mary and the dance world. O'Brien had sent several of Mary's albums to the choreographer Alvin Ailey to gauge his interest in working with Mary's music for his American Dance Theater. In the summer of 1971, Ailey expressed interest in choreographing to *Music for Peace*. Earlier that year, he had choreographed

Leonard Bernstein's *Mass* and had worked with African American sacred music in his decades-long touring production *Revelations*. Commenting on *Music for Peace*, Ailey declared that "what is wonderful about this music is that it is a sum total of Black music, a retrospective."[20] Mary rescored the work, adding her "Old Time Spiritual" from her history of jazz performances at Ailey's request. She also wrote an Agnus Dei, something that Ailey had specifically asked for, as *Music for Peace* did not include this essential part of the Mass Ordinary. To provide Mary with an example of the sound he sought for this movement, Ailey gave Mary recordings of twentieth-century Czech composers. The resulting eerie quality of Mary's *a cappella* "Lamb of God" is markedly different from the remainder of the Mass. Mary also replaced her more subdued "Praise the Lord," which she had used in *Music for Peace*, with her part preaching, part hand clapping "Praise the Lord" from the 1967 Carnegie Hall concert. With Ailey's new title, *Mary Lou's Mass (Dances of Praise)* opened on December 9, 1971, at City Center in New York. The *New York Times* declared, "It is strong and joyful music, with a spirit that cuts across all religious boundaries to provide a celebration of man, God, and peace." Dancers Judith Jamison, who gave a solo performance in Mary's "Our Father," and Dudley Williams, who portrayed Lazarus, were also praised, and Mary and Ailey shared in a "whole-hearted standing ovation."[21]

Mary had performed with a small group of instrumentalists and vocalists for the Ailey premiere. In order for his dance troupe to be able to tour the work, Ailey paid for a recording of Mary's five new Mass movements. Mary permitted Ailey to also use her earlier tracks from *Music for Peace*; Ailey allowed Mary to include the newly recorded movements on her 1975 release *Mary Lou's*

Mass. This new album featured tracks pieces from both the original 1970 recording and the 1972 Ailey session and was reissued in 2005 on Smithsonian Folkways.

* * *

On February 18, 1975, four years after Mary had chased Cardinal Cooke down at Fordham University, *Mary Lou's Mass* was performed at St. Patrick's Cathedral. It was the first jazz Mass to be done at the iconic institution, but the decision to program the work seemingly had little to with Cooke. Msgr. James F. Rigney, the cathedral rector, wanted young people to "feel that they had a claim on the cathedral"[22] and wrote to the heads of local Catholic high schools asking for suggestions to accomplish this purpose. Fr. Thomas Murphy, SJ, president of Regis High School, a Jesuit boys' school located just around the corner from St. Ignatius Loyola Church, suggested that *Mary Lou's Mass* be "given for children at the cathedral." The Mass was not only meant to be for children, of course: Mary herself called the work "a Mass for young-thinking people." But as the *New York Times* critic John S. Wilson pointed out, with the exception of Mary, bassist Buster Williams, and drummer Jerry Griffin, "It will be *by* children."[23] To sing the work, Mary recruited a forty-voice choir comprised of students from Regis High School, the grammar school at Our Lady of Lourdes, Fordham Prep in the Bronx, and the Cathedral High School for Girls. On the day of the Mass, an overflow assembly of 3,000 gathered to pray, clap, and rejoice with Mary's music. Before the service a reporter noted that "one by one the priests came by to say, 'Do your thing, Mary Lou.' "[24] Supported by Mary's trio, the youth sang freely with infectious enthusiasm. Singer Mabel Mercer read the lectionary passage from Isaiah and

Fr. O'Brien gave the homily. Rather than making herself the center of attention, Mary's work did exactly what she had intended: it gathered people of all backgrounds together in love. As one reporter observed, "The cathedral became truly a place for the assembly of the people of God—more than 3,000 of them."[25]

Having *Mary Lou's Mass* at St. Patrick's Cathedral was certainly a milestone in Mary's career. But the many performances of the work that occurred in other churches were just as important. Fr. O'Brien estimated that between 1971 and 1981, fifty performances of the Mass were given each year, usually with Mary at the piano. Although she created a simplified score in 1974 so that others could perform the music, less than a handful of performances of the Mass have been done each year since Mary's death in 1981. In partnership with the Mary Lou Williams Foundation, this author has created a new performance edition of *Mary Lou's Mass* so that churches and choirs can share Mary's joyful music in their own communities. As Mabel Mercer said at St. Patrick's Cathedral in 1975, "I used to think this sort of music didn't belong in church. But now I do. It's just as Isaiah says right here"—she waved the script of her readings—"let the trumpets sound. Everything praises the Lord."[26]

CHAPTER TEN

The Whole Point Is Love (1974–81)

> Mary Lou was . . . a phenomenal presence of universal love.
>
> —Fr. John Dear, interview by the author (July 2019)

In many interviews, Mary referred to 1970 as the point when she "came out [again]." If this declaration doesn't sound new, it wasn't. Staring with her 1957 Newport appearance, the press had heralded Mary's "return" to performing on multiple occasions: in 1964, 1970, and in 1974, when she released *Zoning*, her first instrumental, "nonreligious" recording since the late 1950s. Critics often label 1954–74 as Mary's "religious" period—something separate from the remainder of her work. Yet nothing could be further from the truth. From 1974 until her death in 1981, Mary's outer circumstances simply matched all of the inner work she had done since the mid-1950s. Mary had fully integrated her spirituality, music, and her love of teaching in frequent performances of *Mary Lou's Mass*, history of jazz demonstrations in concerts and classrooms, and her long-standing engagement at the Cookery. Adding more frequent festival and club appearances, ten new albums, and a faculty appointment at Duke University, Mary continued to grow the audience she had been building for over forty years, beginning with her early days with Andy Kirk in the 1930s and '40s through her club, concert, and church appearances in the 1970s.

Mary saw no distinction between "sacred" and "secular" jazz, and performed pieces from her Masses such as "Gloria," "Medi I," and "Medi II" in club settings and on her instrumental albums. Conversely, she included pieces like "O.W.," the bebop instrumental she had written in the 1950s, as a choral prelude in many performances of *Mary Lou's Mass*. As historian Charles Pickeral argues, Mary's liturgical compositions reaffirmed her belief that jazz was spiritual music and had the power to transform lives no matter the context.[1] This conviction underlied all of her output in her final decade.

Mary did "come out again" in the 1970s. This time, more people were able to hear what she had been doing all along.

* * *

Two of Mary's recordings from 1974 and 1976 were revelations to the jazz world, showing that she remained on the cutting edge no matter what style of music she was performing. In 1974, Mary recorded *Zoning*, a modern yet rooted-in-the-blues, stylistically all-encompassing release that stands as one of the most defining albums of her career. Rather than solely focusing on the standard jazz trio of piano, acoustic bass, and drums, Mary swapped out the drum kit for congas on several tracks, alternating two trios with piano solo, piano-bass duo, and duo piano cuts. In a move that predated her historic 1977 Carnegie Hall concert with pianist Cecil Taylor, Mary added a second pianist on two tracks. Zita Carno, a champion of contemporary classical music who had been a friend of saxophonist John Coltrane, joined Mary on "Zoning Fungus II," a new treatment of Mary's atonal piece from the 1950s, "A Fungus Amungus," and on the album's opener, "Intermission." This track begins with a hypnotic odd-meter figure played on electric bass by Bob Cranshaw, who had recently had an injury that prevented him from playing acoustic bass on the session. The instrument fits the of-the-moment early 1970s sound. Drummer Mickey Roker joins in before the piano enters with chords reminiscent of pianist McCoy Tyner before stating the melody in bare-sounding octaves. The whole track runs at just over two minutes in length and piques the listener's curiosity. Mary pares down to a piano-bass duo on Larry Gales's gorgeous ballad "Holy Ghost," which she played at Duke Ellington's funeral in May of that same year. Especially in these stripped-down environments, Mary plays with a sense of stillness and a deft knowledge of when to leave space even in the economy of the duo setting. She revisits "Ghost of Love," her hit from 1938, in a solo rendition and replaces the drums with congas played by Tony Waters on an extended version of "Praise the Lord" and her "Gloria" from *Mary Lou's Mass*. Ranking among the funkiest tracks of all her recordings are "Rosa Mae" and "Play It Momma."

Phyl Garland, who had written consistently about Mary in the *Pittsburgh Courier*, praised the work: "How anyone could sound this fresh after fifty years at the keyboard is almost beyond comprehension. Unlike some of her earlier albums that emphasized message and compositional components, this album focuses on the way she plays—which she does consummately."[2]

In 1976, the Copenhagen-based label Steeplechase released *Free Spirits*, a straight-ahead recording featuring Mary's trio with Buster Williams and Mickey Roker. Unlike *Zoning*, *Free Spirits* includes only one original by Mary, with the remaining tunes composed primarily by other jazz musicians: Buster Williams, trumpeter Miles Davis, pianist Bobby Timmons, and tenor saxophonist John Stubblefield. In live performance in the 1970s, Mary played many of the compositions from *Zoning* and just one from *Free Spirits*: Stubblefield's introspective "Baby Man." With its unhurried tempo and intriguing form that alternates a blues-based melody with chunky choral hits played by the entire trio, the piece fit easily into Mary's experimenting-on-the-blues repertoire.

While these two releases highlighted Mary's pianistic brilliance, Mary also wanted to document her "history of jazz" presentation that she had developed since the late 1950s. Her polished, full program illustrated what she called the "four eras of jazz": spirituals, ragtime, Kansas City swing, and bebop. In late 1970, Mary recorded herself at home on her upright Baldwin piano playing a version of her "history of jazz" concerts. Writing a script that traced her musical career and explained each musical era, Mary began with the spirituals ("Anima Christi"), ragtime ("Who Stole the Lock Off the Henhouse Door"), blues ("My Mama Pinned a Rose on Me"), and several other examples before closing with what she labels as "modern" ("Medi I," her slow blues from *Mary Lou's Mass*). In 1978, Moe Asch released the recording as *The History of Jazz* on Folkways and included Mary's script as an insert. This album is the clearest representation of Mary's interpretation of jazz history available on record, complete with Mary's voice, and is available at the Smithsonian Folkways website.

A year prior to *The History of Jazz*, Folkways released *The Asch Recordings: 1944–47*, a compilation of Mary's mid-1940s recordings for Moe Asch. This wealth of recorded output after decades of relatively few appearances on wax confirmed Mary's stature not only as a legendary jazz artist but as a musician who remained consistently modern no matter the decade. One reviewer wrote, "To move from the Folkways set [*Asch 1944–47*] to *Free Spirits* is to be nearly overwhelmed by the scope of Mary Lou Williams' musicality. . . . Somehow she seems to be saying that there is an unbroken thread running from spirituals and blues through [pianist] McCoy Tyner."[3]

Mary envisioned a new way to represent this "unbroken thread" of jazz history. Contacting her old friend David Stone Martin, the two created a drawing of a tree titled "History of Jazz." The roots of the sturdy tree are labeled "suffering," while the sides of the trunk are lined by the blues. Extending from the roots to the branches are spirituals, ragtime, Kansas City swing, and bop, Mary's jazz eras. Each branch is filled with names of musicians totaling more than ninety in all, including Thomas "Fats" Waller, Art Tatum, and Charlie Parker. Jutting out to the left are several stunted, bare branches labeled "commercial rock," "black magic," "avant guard [garde]," "cults," "exercises," and "classical books," reflecting Mary's beliefs that rock was destroying jazz and that jazz could not be learned out of books.

Mary's persistence in sharing the history of jazz stemmed from her conviction that jazz was "healing to the soul" and needed to be experienced by as many people, in as many environments, as possible. She was especially concerned for

African American young people who, she said, knew Diana Ross but not Billie Holiday. In order to "save jazz," Mary decided to mount another Carnegie Hall concert. As opposed to her 1955 Bel Canto extravaganza, for this performance she had only two musicians on stage: herself and avant-garde pianist Cecil Taylor in a program entitled *Embraced: A Concert of New Music for Two Pianos Exploring the History of Jazz with Love*. Many were intrigued that Mary, still perceived as part of an older tradition, would choose to play with Taylor, a pioneer of "free jazz," a type of improvisation that did not rely on preexisting song structure or chord progressions but was created spontaneously in the moment. The pairing seemed all the more surprising since Mary herself had spent years railing against the avant-garde movement, even naming it as one of her stunted "tree of jazz" branches. But in the liner notes to the live recording of the concert, Mary emphasized that "the feeling of the Blues is characteristic of good Jazz no matter what form it takes"[4] and included Taylor in that estimation. Describing her experience of hearing Taylor perform at Ronnie Scott's Jazz Club several years earlier, Mary wrote, "I felt great warmth from him. Being a creative and searching kind of musician, such as I am, Cecil thrilled me with his integrity and originality. I call him 'my Giant of the Avant-Garde.' "[5] Taylor had been a fan of Mary's playing for decades. After first hearing her in 1951 as a conservatory student in Boston, he saw her perform her six years later at the Newport Jazz Festival. He was a regular listener at Mary's long-standing duo gig at the Cookery where he praised her, saying, "No one's playing anything but you." It was clear that both pianists admired each other's work.

Yet even with their mutual admiration, tension heightened between the two pianists as the Carnegie Hall date approached.

Mary wanted to use her "history of jazz" approach in the first half and have Taylor provide short musical themes for improvisation in the second half. Mary claimed that Taylor had agreed to this plan, but when she gave him sheet music for her tunes, he refused to use the scores. Wanting to add a rhythm section on several pieces, Mary hired Bob Cranshaw and Mickey Roker without asking Taylor who he would like to have on bass and drums, only adding to the friction.

When listening to the live recording, it is virtually impossible to imagine how Mary could have held her ground both musically and personally for the seventy-five-minute concert. She managed to play five of her "history of jazz" pieces starting with her original spiritual, "The Lord Is Heavy," demonstrating ragtime, boogie-woogie, Kansas City swing, and bebop, but her sound was often covered up by Taylor's continuous playing. While Mary occasionally stopped and tried to find moments to respond to Taylor's up and down the entire range of the keyboard, Taylor left so little room for interaction that it was Mary who had to make all of the decisions regarding how to start or end a tune. On their fifth piece, which included Mary's "Roll 'Em," Mary yelled, "Wait for the break!" before the bass and drums entered. On the second half where Taylor provided his own musical themes as an improvisational springboard, he played with more of a dynamic range, getting more colors out of the piano. While there were several moments of musical dialogue, on listening to the recording, it sounds as if one is hearing a loud person talking in a separate room who Mary has to fight in order to get a word in edgewise. After the final selection, "Back to the Blues," Fr. O'Brien had to push Mary back out onstage to play three encores—without Taylor. Closing with a standard she had performed for decades, "I Can't Get Started," the audience responded with more abandon than they had expressed throughout the entire evening, as if they, like the two pianists, had been waiting for a moment of rest.

Soon after the concert, Mary received an opportunity to present her philosophy of jazz in a manner she had never thought possible. In the summer of 1977, she accepted an invitation from Frank Tirro, head of the music department at Duke University, to teach as an artist-in-residence for the 1977–78 school year. Though keeping her Harlem apartment, Mary bought a nine-room, four-bedroom home in Durham, North Carolina, the first house she had ever owned. Receiving a steady salary, Mary experienced financial stability for the first time in her sixty-year career. Her teaching duties consisted of coaching the college jazz ensemble and teaching an introduction to jazz class; her contract was extended for three more years. After just one semester, Mary became so popular that more than 750 students signed up for her class, which was designed to hold eighty. Co-teaching the class with Fr. O'Brien, the two accepted 180 students. The peace activist Fr. John Dear, then a Duke student, wanted to enroll in Mary's class as a sophomore, but only seniors were allowed to register for the class. Knowing that O'Brien was a Jesuit, Dear approached him, explaining that he had attended a Jesuit high school and simply had to take Mary's class. O'Brien let Dear in for the fall semester. Dear never forgot his first impression of Mary, describing her late entrance into a large symphony rehearsal room with a "massive black piano" where students were waiting for her arrival. Dear recalled:

> She walked in the room. I've never seen anyone like her from then until now. . . . She had this massive black hair,

> and she's all dressed in black . . . black stockings, black shoes, and she's got this big black papier mâché rose . . . on the left side of her dress. . . . The kids at Duke had never seen the likes of this. She came sauntering in like she had all the time in the whole world, like she was Queen Elizabeth. . . . She walked ten yards from the door to the piano and she takes like ten minutes to get there. . . . . She had us in the palm of her hand. She gets to the piano and she sits down and she's just got her left hand there, and she starts boogie-woogie. . . . She goes on for an hour, doesn't say anything, and then says, "Jazz is LOVE. And I'm here to teach you LOVE through jazz." . . . Then she got up and walked out of the room. You could have knocked me over with a feather.[6]

Dear took lessons from Mary at her home and also sang in a student choir that Mary formed for a 1978 CBS television special, *Christmas Eve with Mary Lou Williams at Duke University*. He credits Mary with changing his life. While at Duke, Dear underwent a conversion and decided to become a Jesuit priest. He considers Mary to be "one of the greatest people I ever knew, hands down. To me, she was the embodiment of universal, unconditional love. And I knew Mother Teresa pretty well. When I was with Mother Teresa, I would think, 'Wow, this is Mary Lou Williams.' "[7]

Away from campus, Mary was active at Holy Cross Church, a local African American Catholic parish, and played *Mary Lou's Mass* there in a liturgy with Duke students. At the university, she performed at quarterly alumni parties but preferred to spend her free time with several close friends, including a student, Marsha Vick, who took piano lessons at Mary's home on the old Baldwin upright that had been a fixture in her Harlem apartment. The Baldwin company soon provided a grand piano for Mary's home for an *Ebony* feature article. For two years, Mary had corresponded with writer Phyl Garland, asking when she would be coming to Durham to write a feature on her. Mary explained that while her class at Duke was extremely popular, it was mostly white students who were signing up, and she thought that an *Ebony* feature would help Black students to become aware of their great American jazz heritage. Garland did visit Mary and wrote an extensive article on her which appeared in the October 1979 issue, including pictures of Mary at home at the Baldwin grand and in her classroom at Duke.

Even with her teaching responsibilities, Mary continued to travel and record. In October 1978, she recorded a performance-interview for pianist Marian McPartland's new public radio program, *Piano Jazz*. McPartland had always admired Mary and invited her to be her first studio guest for this hour-long program of piano solo, duo, and conversation. Although McPartland had explained that the show was to feature piano without a rhythm section, Mary brought bassist Ronnie Boykins with her to the taping in New York, defying McPartland's directive. In their conversation, Mary sounded hostile throughout much of the program. After Mary opened with her "Space Playing Blues," McPartland asked, "How do you explain this to your kids when you play a chord [she then played a dissonant chord] like that?" Mary replied, "I didn't play a chord like that. I just tell them the chord: E-flat nine with a flat five."[8] Although the tension between the two pianists was palpable throughout the show, both contributed significant musical moments on "Caravan" and "The Jeep is Jumpin'." But when the series aired the following April, it was pianist Billy Taylor, and not Mary, who was the guest on the first episode.

Even after Mary was diagnosed with bladder cancer in February of 1979, she continued to travel, alternating bouts in the hospital with engagements in Washington, DC; São Paulo, Brazil; and New York. In the spring of 1979, she played for a second time at St. Patrick's Cathedral as part of its centennial celebration, performing *Mary Lou's Mass* with a choir from Fordham Prep in the Bronx. The following spring she felt well enough to travel with Fr. O'Brien to Kansas City on a birthday trip, where she received an honorary degree at Rockhurst College. She also coached the Clark College Jazz Ensemble on a visit to her home state of Georgia for the Atlanta Jazz Festival. Filmmaker Joanne Burke captured Mary in both of these settings in her documentary *Music on My Mind*, showing Mary meeting her half brother Willis in Atlanta, demonstrating how to create a big band arrangement on the spot during a television interview, and conversing with musicians who had played with her, including Dizzy Gillespie and saxophonist Buddy Tate. The film shows a radiant Mary, at home with students and on the bandstand, all in the final year of her life.

On October 23, 1980, Mary taught her final full day of classes at Duke. She checked into the hospital a week later for a month of radiation treatments and tests. Mary had a piano delivered to her room so that she could continue working on a piece she was writing for Duke's wind symphony. In and out of the hospital over the next several months, she received an unexpected visitor. Now a college senior, John Dear had volunteered with the hospital priest to bring daily Communion to dying patients. Receiving the list of patients to visit, Dear was shocked to see Mary's name. He began visiting Mary regularly until she transitioned to hospice care, sitting with her and asking her to tell her life story, something she had always loved to do. Mary spoke about her visions of Martin de Porres, performing at Billie Holiday's funeral, and her friendship with Fr. Woods. Eventually,

Dear started bringing religious questions to Mary, asking, "Who is God? What do you think of Jesus?" He wrote down Mary's reply: "Forget it all, John. The whole point is love."[9]

While Mary was in hospice at home on her birthday of May 8, 1981, Duke University president Terry Sanford paid a visit and presented her with the Trinity Award, an honor bestowed upon the most beloved faculty member. Mary confessed to her friend and student Marsha Vick that the award "touched me more than any award I've gotten since I've been playin'."[10] Three weeks later, on May 28, Mary died at home. On June 1, her funeral was held in New York at her baptismal parish of St. Ignatius Loyola Church. Fr. O'Brien gave the homily, Br. Mario was one of the lectors, and Mary received solo musical tributes from Dizzy Gillespie and Marian McPartland. Vocalist Carmen Lundy led the New York Boys Choir in singing "Praise the Lord" from *Mary Lou's Mass*. The following day in her Pittsburgh childhood neighborhood of East Liberty, Mary's funeral Mass was celebrated at St. Peter and Paul Catholic Church. Her body was laid to rest in Calvary Cemetery, four miles south in Hazelwood.

* * *

Mary wanted jazz to be heard on the sidewalk, in churches, nightclubs, community centers, and schools: in short, everywhere. She recognized that jazz had the power to transform lives and to heal individuals and communities. A year before her death, she established the Mary Lou Williams Foundation to help bring jazz to young people. The organization still exists and is currently working to make Mary's sheet music catalog of more than 350 compositions more readily available. A new performance edition of *Mary Lou's Mass* is newly available so that churches, choirs, and colleges can share Mary's music in concert and in liturgy, continuing to spread her gospel that "jazz is love."

A quote from Mary at the close of the film *Music on My Mind* sums up her life's work: "Music has always been my entire life. The earth is in need of true jazz. We need this for survival. We should keep our minds and hearts on music. Who knows? Our playing may be our freedom for ourselves and others."[11]

Notes

Introduction—pages 1–6

1. John Williams, quoted in Linda Dahl, *Morning Glory: A Biography of Mary Lou Williams* (New York: Pantheon Books, 1999), 246. Used by permission of Linda Dahl.

Chapter One—pages 7–15

1. Mary Lou Williams, quoted in Linda Dahl, *Morning Glory: A Biography of Mary Lou Williams* (New York: Pantheon Books, 1999), 17. Used by permission of Linda Dahl.
2. Williams, quoted in Dahl, 15. Used by permission of Linda Dahl.
3. Mary Lou Williams, "Jazzspeak," disc 2, track 10, on *Nite Life*, recorded 1971, released 1998, Chiaroscuro Records, 2:39.
4. Mary Lou Williams, "Jazz Oral History Project," interview by John S. Wilson, National Endowment for the Arts/Institute of Jazz Studies, Rutgers University, transcript (IJS.0119), July 26, 1977, 107, https://doi.org/10.7282/T3JH3Q2Z.
5. Williams, "Jazz Oral History Project," 13.
6. Max Jones, *Jazz Talking: Profiles, Interviews, and Other Riffs on Jazz Musicians* (New York: Da Capo Press, 2000), 179.
7. Mary Lou Williams, quoted in Dahl, *Morning Glory*, 34.
8. John Williams, quoted in Dahl, 44.
9. Mary Lou Williams, quoted in Dahl, 44.

Chapter Two—pages 16–27

1. Max Jones, *Jazz Talking: Profiles, Interviews, and Other Riffs on Jazz Musicians* (New York: Da Capo Press, 2000), 183.

2. Jones, 187.

3. Andy Kirk, as told to Amy Lee, *Twenty Years on Wheels* (Ann Arbor: University of Michigan Press, 1989), 71.

4. Jack Kapp, quoted in Kirk, 72.

5. Mary Lou Williams, quoted in Linda Dahl, *Morning Glory: A Biography of Mary Lou Williams* (New York: Pantheon Books, 1999), 76. Used by permission of Linda Dahl.

6. Williams, quoted in Dahl, 79.

7. Jones, *Jazz Talking*, 190.

8. Sam Stiefel, quoted in Dahl, *Morning Glory*, 81. Used by permission of Linda Dahl.

9. Mary Lou Williams, quoted in Dahl, 85. Used by permission of Linda Dahl.

10. Jones, *Jazz Talking*, 192.

11. Jack Kapp, quoted in Kirk, *Twenty Years on Wheels*, 84.

12. Jones, *Jazz Talking*, 191.

13. Mary Lou Williams, quoted in Dahl, *Morning Glory*, 109. Used by permission of Linda Dahl.

14. David Kane, "Mary Lou Williams, Foremost Female Swing Pianist, Shuns News Reporters," *Pittsburgh Courier* (November 13, 1937): 21.

15. Mary Lou Williams/Henry Wells, "Little Joe from Chicago," February 8, 1938, Decca Records.

16. Jones, *Jazz Talking*, 198.

17. Kirk, *Twenty Years on Wheels*, 73.

18. Kirk, 110.

Chapter Three—pages 28–40

1. "The Injured: Riot List of Injured and Dead," *New York Amsterdam News* (August 7, 1943): 7.

2. "Rumors of Soldier's 'Killing' Caused Frenzied Mob to Riot," *New York Amsterdam News* (August 7, 1943): 4.

3. "The Injured: Riot List of Injured and Dead," 7.

4. Fiorello La Guardia, quoted in Farah Jasmine Griffin, *Harlem Nocturne: Women Artists and Progressive Politics During World War II* (New York: Basic *Civitas* Books, 2013), 95.

5. "No Kitten on the Keys," *Time* (July 26, 1943): 78.

6. Mary Lou Williams, "Jazz Oral History Project," John S. Wilson interview, National Endowment for the Arts/Institute of Jazz Studies, Rutgers University, transcript (IJS.0119), July 26, 1977, 130, https://doi.org/10.7282/T3JH3Q2Z.

7. Griffin, *Harlem Nocturne*, 178.

8. Susan Reed, quoted in Barney Josephson with Terry Trilling-Josephson, *Cafe Society: The Wrong Place for the Right People* (Urbana: University of Illinois Press, 2015), 176.

9. Mary Lou Williams, liner notes to the *Zodiac Suite* (New York: Asch Records, 1945; Smithsonian Folkways, 1995).

10. Barry Ulanov, "Concert Spree," *Metronome* 62, no. 2 (February 1946): 18.

11. Melba Liston Archives, Columbia College Chicago/Center for Black Music Research.

12. Mary Lou Williams, "Music and Progress," *Jazz Record*, no. 60 (November 1947): 23–24.

13. Mary Lou Williams, Autobiographical Notebook #3, 375, Mary Lou Williams Collection (IJS.0119), MC 60, Series 5, Box 1, Folder 4, Institute of Jazz Studies, Rutgers University, Newark, NJ.

14. Williams, 375.

15. Griffin, *Harlem Nocturne*, 192; Williams, Autobiographical Notebook #3, 378.

Chapter Four—pages 41–48

1. Mary Lou Williams, quoted in Linda Dahl, *Morning Glory: A Biography of Mary Lou Williams* (New York: Pantheon Books, 1999), 241. Used by permission of Linda Dahl.

2. Max Jones, quoted in Dahl, 225.

3. Nat Hentoff, "Mary Lou Still Learning, Teaching and Progressing," *DownBeat* 19, no. 25 (December 17, 1952): 7.

4. Mark Nevard, ". . . And Mary Lou on LP," *Melody Maker* (February 7, 1953): 5.

5. Edgar Jackson, letter in "More MM Critics Enter the Fray: Mary Lou," *Melody Maker* (February 21, 1953): 8.

6. Dill Jones, letter to "Melody Mailbag," *Melody Maker* (February 14, 1953): 5.

7. Robert Gottlieb, ed., *Reading Jazz: A Gathering of Autobiography, Reportage, and Criticism from 1919 to Now* (New York: Vintage Books, 1999), 87–116.

8. Mary Lou Williams, quoted in Dahl, *Morning Glory*, 236. Used by permission of Linda Dahl.

9. Mary Lou Williams, "What I Learned from God about Jazz," *Sepia* (April 1958): 57.

Chapter Five—pages 49–62

1. Mary Lou Williams, "Jazz Oral History Project," interview by John S. Wilson, National Endowment for the Arts/Institute of Jazz Studies, Rutgers University, transcript (IJS.0119), July 26, 1977, 142, https://doi.org/10.7282/T3JH3Q2Z.

2. Williams, 142.

3. Farah Jasmine Griffin, *Harlem Nocturne: Women Artists and Progressive Politics during World War II* (New York: Basic *Civitas* Books, 2013), 178.

4. Mary Lou Williams, quoted in Linda Dahl, *Morning Glory: A Biography of Mary Lou Williams* (New York: Pantheon Books, 1999), 246. Used by permission of Linda Dahl.

5. Williams, "Jazz Oral History Project," 149.

6. Williams, 146.

7. Bobbie Ferguson, interview by the author, December 2018.

8. Williams, "Jazz Oral History Project," 146.

9. Williams, 145.

10. Williams, 146.

11. Mary Lou Williams, quoted in Dahl, *Morning Glory*, 257.

12. Williams, "Jazz Oral History Project," 155.

13. Dizzy Gillespie with Al Fraser, *To Be, or Not . . . to Bop* (Garden City, NY: Doubleday, 1979), 425.

14. Mitch Finley, "Barry Ulanov: 'I Remember Tom with Great Fondness,'" *Merton Seasonal* (March 2019): 6.

15. Williams, "Jazz Oral History Project," 148.

16. Fr. C. J. McNaspy, "The Miracle on 16th Street," *America* 107, no. 25 (September 22, 1962): 793.

17. Fr. Anthony Woods, quoted in Marian McPartland, "Into the Sun," *DownBeat*, August 27, 1964. Reprinted in Marian McPartland, *All in Good Time* (New York: Oxford University Press, 1987), 67.

18. Fr. John Dear, quoted in Dahl, *Morning Glory*, 260.

19. Melba Liston, quoted in Tammy L. Kernodle, *Soul on Soul: The Life and Music of Mary Lou Williams*, 1st ed. (Boston: Northeastern University Press, 2004), 188.

20. Fr. Anthony Woods, quoted in Whitney Balliett, "Out Here Again," originally published in *The New Yorker* (May 2, 1964): 54. Reprinted in *American Musicians: Fifty-Six Portraits in Jazz* (New York: Oxford University Press, 1986), 107.

21. Lewis K. McMillan Jr., "Grand Lady of Jazz," *Musical Journal* (September 1974): 51.

22. Dizzy Gillespie and his orchestra, *Dizzy Gillespie & Mary Lou Williams at Newport*, recorded at the Newport Jazz Festival, July 6, 1957, Verve MGV-8244, 1958, 33⅓ rpm. Remastered on *Dizzy Gillespie at Newport*, Verve 314 513 754-2, 1992, compact disc.

23. Mary Lou Williams, "What I Learned from God about Jazz," *Sepia* (April 1958): 59.

24. Williams, 59.

25. "Pianist's Return," *Time* (September 16, 1957): 78.

26. Marian McPartland, "Mary Lou Williams: A Return," *DownBeat* 24, no. 21 (October 17, 1957): 12.

27. Williams, "Jazz Oral History Project," 151.

28. Williams, 152.

Chapter Six—pages 63–71

1. Linda Dahl, *Morning Glory: A Biography of Mary Lou Williams* (New York: Pantheon Books, 1999), 265.

2. Whitney Balliett, "Out Here Again," originally published in *The New Yorker* (May 2, 1964): 80; reprinted in *American Musicians: Fifty-Six Portraits in Jazz* (New York: Oxford University Press, 1986).

3. Vaughn A. Booker, *Lift Every Voice and Swing: Black Musicians and Religious Culture in the Jazz Century* (New York: New York University Press, 2020): 226.

4. Dizzy Gillespie, interview in *Music on My Mind*, directed by Joanne Burke, produced by Joanne Burke and the Film and Video Workshop (1988).

5. Booker, *Lift Every Voice and Swing*, 215.

6. Fr. Norman Weyand, review of *The Junkie Priest*, by John D. Harris, *Review for Religious* 23, no. 5 (September 1964): 667.

7. Br. Mario Hancock, quoted in Dahl, *Morning Glory*, 268.

8. Russ Wilson, "Caught in the Act," *DownBeat* 29, no. 8 (April 12, 1962): 37.

9. Tom O'Leary, "That's Entertainment," *The Monitor* (February 9, 1962): 11.

10. Mary Lou Williams Collection (IJS.0119), MC 60, Sister Martha Mulligan, Subseries 3D: Correspondence with Religious, Box 21, Folder 1, Institute of Jazz Studies, Rutgers University, Newark, NJ.

Chapter Seven—pages 72–84

1. Fr. John Dear, interview by the author, July 2019.

2. "Negro Saint's Day Held Blow to Racism," *New York Times* (November 4, 1962): 48.

3. "St. Martin 'Rebuke' to Racist," *Advocate* (November 8, 1962): 24.

4. "Pianist Composes Jazz Hymn in Honor of Negro St. Martin," *The Bridgeport Telegram* (October 31, 1962): 5.

5. Stanley Dance, "Jazz," *Music Journal* 21 (1963): 109–10.

6. Gérard Pochonet, liner notes to *Mary Lou Williams Presents Black Christ of the Andes* (New York: Mary Records, 1964; rereleased by Smithsonian Folkways, 2004).

7. Fr. Peter O'Brien, liner notes to reissue of *Black Christ of the Andes* (Smithsonian Folkways, 2004).

8. Phyl Garland, "Gift of Beauty," *Pittsburgh Courier* (August 1, 1964): 13.

9. "Jazz: The Prayerful One," *Time* (February 21, 1964): 58.

10. O'Brien, liner notes to reissue of *Black Christ of the Andes*.

11. Mary Lou Williams Collection (IJS.0119), MC 60, John J. Wright, Subseries 3D: Correspondence with Religious, Box 21, Folder 14, Institute of Jazz Studies, Rutgers University, Newark, NJ.

12. Williams Collection, MC 60, Fr. Michael P. Williams, Subseries 3D: Correspondence with Religious, Box 21, Folder 12.

13. Constitution on the Sacred Liturgy, https://www.vatican.va/archive/hist_councils/ii_vatican_council/documents/vat-ii_const_19631204_sacrosanctum-concilium_en.html.

14. Roy Kohler, "Pittsburgh Jazz Renaissance," *Pittsburgh Press* (June 14, 1964): 129.

15. George Wein, quoted in Carl Apone, "All That Jazz Is Great at Arena," *Pittsburgh Press* (June 20, 1964): 2.

16. Stanley Dance, "Jazz in Pittsburgh," *Saturday Review* (July 11, 1964): 43.

17. Williams Collection, MC 60, Fr. Michael P. Williams, Subseries 3D: Correspondence with Religious, Box 21, Folder 12.

18. Fr. Norman Weyand, quoted in Apone, "All That Jazz Is Great at Arena," 2.

19. Williams Collection, MC 60, Fr. Norman Weyand, Subseries 3D: Correspondence with Religious, Box 21, Folder 11.

20. Williams Collection, Fr. Weyand.

21. Billy Taylor, liner notes to *The Jazz Piano* (Mosaic Records, 1965).

22. Williams Collection, MC 60, Fr. John Ayoob, Subseries 3D: Correspondence with Religious, Box 19, Folder 3.

Chapter Eight—pages 85–98

1. Gemma Biggi, quoted in Linda Dahl, *Morning Glory: A Biography of Mary Lou Williams* (New York: Pantheon Books, 1999), 287.

2. Mary Lou Williams Collection (IJS.0119), MC 60, Fr. Norman Weyand, Subseries 3D: Correspondence with Religious, Box 21, Folder 11, Institute of Jazz Studies, Rutgers University, Newark, NJ.

3. Williams Collection, MC 60, Br. Mario Hancock, Subseries 3D: Correspondence with Religious, Box 19, Folder 14.

4. Williams Collection, Br. Hancock.

5. "Jazz: The Prayerful One," *Time* (February 21, 1964): 59.

6. Rebecca Sullivan, *Visual Habits: Nuns, Feminism, and American Postwar Popular Culture* (Toronto: University of Toronto Press, 2005), 170.

7. *Catholic News Service*, "Liturgy Document," January 6, 1967, issued by the Press Department, U.S. Catholic Conference.

8. Robert C. Doty, "Jazz Mass Included in Ban by Vatican on 'Strange' Rites," *New York Times* (January 7, 1967): 1.

9. Fr. C. J. McNaspy, "Liturgy and Headlines," *America* (January 21, 1967): 79.

10. *New York Amsterdam News* (January 28, 1967): 12.

11. *New York Amsterdam News* (February 4, 1967): 7.

12. *New York Amsterdam News*, 16, 18.

13. Fr. C. J. McNaspy, "Eternal and Everyday," *America* (February 25, 1967): 292.

14. Mary Lou Williams, quoted in Dahl, *Morning Glory*, 290. Used by permission of Linda Dahl.

15. Williams Collection, MC 60, Fr. Michael P. Williams, Subseries 3D: Correspondence with Religious, Box 21, Folder 12.

16. John S. Wilson, "Mary Lou Takes Her Jazz Mass to Church," *New York Times* (February 9, 1975): 120.

17. Mary Lou Williams, quoted in Dahl, *Morning Glory*, 293. Used by permission of Linda Dahl.

18. "SSCA Mass Will Feature Subtle New Jazz Music," *Pittsburgh Catholic* (July 20, 1967): 9.

19. Williams Collection, MC 60, Br. Mario Hancock, Subseries 3D: Correspondence with Religious, Box 19, Folder 14.

20. Williams Collection, Br. Hancock.

21. Williams Collection, MC 60, Fr. Bob Ledogar, Subseries 3D: Correspondence with Religious, Box 20, Folder 8.

22. Williams Collection, Fr. Ledogar.

23. Mary Lou Williams and Fr. Robert Ledogar, "Kyrie," from *Mass for the Lenten Season*, 1968.

24. Letter from Omer Westendorf to Fr. Robert Ledogar, January 16, 1968, Schomburg Center for Research in Black Culture, Manuscripts, Archives and Rare Books Division, Eddie Bonnemère Papers, Box 2.

25. Dorothy Day, "On Pilgrimage," *Catholic Worker* (March 1968): 1.

26. Letter from Mary Lou Williams to Dorothy Day, March 17, 1968, Dorothy Day-Catholic Worker Collection, Series D-1, Box 22, Folder 6, Marquette University, Milwaukee, WI.

27. Letter from Williams to Day.

28. Dorothy Day, "On Pilgrimage," *Catholic Worker* (April 1968): 1.

29. Mary Lou Williams, "Tell Him Not to Talk Too Long," as recorded on *Mary Lou's Mass*, Mary Records, 1975; re-released on Smithsonian Folkways, 2005.

30. Letter from Williams to Day, April 16, 1968, Dorothy Day-Catholic Worker Collection, Series D-1, Box 22, Folder 6, Marquette University, Milwaukee, WI.

Chapter Nine—pages 99–114

1. Dutch Jazz Orchestra, *Rediscovered Music of Mary Lou Williams: The Lady Who Swings the Band* (Challenge Records CR73251, 2005).

2. Mary Lou Williams letter to Dorothy Day, October 14, 1968, Dorothy Day-Catholic Worker Collection, Series D-1, Box 22, Folder 6, Marquette University, Milwaukee, WI.

3. Mary Lou Williams Collection (IJS.0119), MC 60, Br. Mario Hancock, Subseries 3D: Correspondence with Religious, Box 19, Folder 14, Institute of Jazz Studies, Rutgers University, Newark, NJ.

4. Williams Collection, Br. Hancock.

5. Thomas Merton, quoted in David Brent Johnson, "The Jazz Monk: Thomas Merton," April 12, 2017, https://indianapublicmedia.org/nightlights/soul-swing-jazz-religion.php.

6. Williams Collection, Williams to Hancock, January 7, 1969.

7. Louis Panarale, "TV Cameras Upset Plans for Jazz Mass," NC News Service (foreign) issued by the Press Department, U.S. Catholic Conference (February 3, 1969): 15.

8. Williams Collection, Br. Hancock.

9. Panarale, "TV Cameras Upset Plans for Jazz Mass," 15.

10. Panarale, 15.

11. Mary Lou Williams, quoted in Linda Dahl, *Morning Glory: A Biography of Mary Lou Williams* (New York: Pantheon Books, 1999), 306. Used by permission of Linda Dahl.

12. Williams Collection, Br. Hancock.

13. Williams Collection, Br. Hancock.

14. Mary Lou Williams, quoted in Dahl, *Morning Glory*, 307.

15. Mary Lou Williams, "People in Trouble," as recorded on *Music for Peace*, 1970, Mary Records, and re-released on *Mary Lou's Mass*, Smithsonian Folkways, 2005.

16. Leon Thomas, "One,"as recorded on *Mary Lou's Mass* (originally titled "The World" on *Music for Peace*, Mary Records, 1970).

17. Mary Lou Williams, quoted in Dahl, *Morning Glory*, 314. Used by permission of Linda Dahl.

18. "Mary Lou Takes Her Jazz Mass to Church," *New York Times* (February 9, 1975): 120.

19. Barney Josephson with Terry Trilling-Josephson, *Cafe Society: The Wrong Place for the Right People* (Urbana: University of Illinois Press, 2015), 276.

20. Anna Kisselgoff, "Ailey Dancers to Give 'Mary Lou's Mass,' " *New York Times* (December 9, 1971): 62.

21. Clive Barnes, "Ballet: Ailey Company Dances 'Mary Lou's Mass,' " *New York Times* (December 11, 1971): 23.

22. "Mary Lou Takes Her Jazz Mass to Church," 120.

23. "Mary Lou Takes Her Jazz Mass to Church," 120.

24. Nancy Q. Keefe, "Mary Lou's Mass," *Berkshire Eagle* (February 28, 1975): 6.

25. Keefe, 6.

26. Keefe, 6.

Chapter Ten—pages 115–27

1. Charles W. Pickeral, "The Masses of Mary Lou Williams: The Evolution of a Liturgical Style" (PhD diss., Texas Tech University, 1998), http://search.proquest.com/docview/304454139/abstract/1D6C12B4B5964688PQ/1.

2. Phyl Garland, "Sounds," *Ebony* 29, no. 12 (October 1974): 30.

3. Tom Piazza, "Mary Lou Williams: The Asch Recordings; Mary Lou Williams: Free Spirits," *Jazz Magazine* 2, no. 2 (Winter 1978): 64.

4. Mary Lou Williams, liner notes to *Embraced: A Concert of New Music for Two Pianos Exploring the History of Jazz with Love* (Pablo Records 2620 108, 1978).

5. Williams, liner notes to *Embraced*.

6. Fr. John Dear, interview by the author, July 2019.

7. Fr. Dear, interview.

8. Mary Lou Williams, *Marian McPartland's Piano Jazz* radio program (recorded in 1978, released on compact disc on the Jazz Alliance, TJA-12045-2, 2004).

9. Fr. Dear, interview.

10. Mary Lou Williams, quoted in Linda Dahl, *Morning Glory: A Biography of Mary Lou Williams* (New York: Pantheon Books, 1999), 367.

11. Mary Lou Williams, interview in *Music on My Mind*, directed by Joanne Burke, produced by Joanne Burke and the Film and Video Workshop (1988).

Selected Bibliography

Books

Balliett, Whitney. *American Musicians: Fifty-Six Portraits in Jazz.* New York: Oxford University Press, 1986.

Booker, Vaughn A. *Lift Every Voice and Swing: Black Musicians and Religious Culture in the Jazz Century*. New York: New York University Press, 2020.

Buehrer, Theodore E., ed. *Mary Lou Williams: Selected Works for Big Band*. Music of the United States of America, vol. 25. Middleton, WI: A-R Editions, 2013.

Burke, Patrick. *Come In and Hear the Truth: Jazz and Race on 52nd Street*. Chicago: University of Chicago Press, 2008.

Burrows, George. *The Recordings of Andy Kirk and His Clouds of Joy*. New York: Oxford University Press, 2019.

Dahl, Linda. *Morning Glory: A Biography of Mary Lou Williams*. New York: Pantheon Books, 1999.

de Barros, Paul. *Shall We Play That One Together? The Life and Art of Jazz Piano Legend Marian McPartland*. New York: St. Martin's Press, 2012.

Driggs, Frank, and Chuck Haddix. *Kansas City Jazz: From Ragtime to Bebop—A History.* New York: Oxford University Press, 2005.

Edwards, Brent Hayes. *Epistrophies: Jazz and the Literary Imagination*. Cambridge, MA: Harvard University Press, 2017.

Feather, Leonard. *The Jazz Years: Earwitness to an Era*. New York: Da Capo Press, 1987.

Foley, Edward. *A Lyrical Vision: The Music Documents of the US Bishops*. Eugene, OR: Wipf and Stock, 2009.

Gillespie, Dizzy, with Al Fraser. *To Be, or Not . . . to Bop*. Garden City, NY: Doubleday, 1979.

Gottlieb, Robert, ed. *Reading Jazz: A Gathering of Autobiography, Reportage, and Criticism from 1919 to Now*. New York: Vintage Books, 1999.

Griffin, Farah Jasmine. *Harlem Nocturne: Women Artists and Progressive Politics during World War II*. New York: Basic *Civitas* Books, 2013.

Jones, Max. *Jazz Talking: Profiles, Interviews, and Other Riffs on Jazz Musicians*. New York: Da Capo Press, 2000.

Josephson, Barney, with Terry Trilling-Josephson. *Cafe Society: The Wrong Place for the Right People*. Urbana: University of Illinois Press, 2015.

Kenney, Williams Howland. *Jazz on the River*. Chicago: University of Chicago Press, 2005.

Kernodle, Tammy L. *Soul on Soul: The Life and Music of Mary Lou Williams*. 1st ed. Boston: Northeastern University Press, 2004.

Kirk, Andy, as told to Amy Lee. *Twenty Years on Wheels*. Ann Arbor: University of Michigan Press, 1989.

Lawrence, Jack. *They All Sang My Songs*. Fort Lee, NJ: Barricade Books, 2004.

McPartland, Marian. *All in Good Time*. New York: Oxford University Press, 1987.

Myers, Marc. *Why Jazz Happened*. Berkeley: University of California Press, 2013.

Schuller, Gunther. *The Swing Era: The Development of Jazz, 1930–1945*. New York: Oxford University Press, 1989.

Shaw, Arnold. *52nd Street: The Street of Jazz*. New York, Da Capo Press, 1977.

Sullivan, Rebecca. *Visual Habits: Nuns, Feminism, and American Postwar Popular Culture*. Toronto: University of Toronto Press, 2005.

Ulanov, Barry. *A Handbook of Jazz*. London: Hutchison, 1958.

Ulanov, Barry. *A History of Jazz in America*. New York: Viking Press, 1952 (3rd printing, 1955).

Unterbrink, Mary. *Jazz Women at the Keyboard*. Jefferson, NC: McFarland, 1983.

Whitaker, Mark. *Smoketown: The Untold Story of the Other Great Black Renaissance*. New York: Simon & Schuster, 2019.

Dissertations

Pickeral, Charles W. "The Masses of Mary Lou Williams: The Evolution of a Liturgical Style." PhD dissertation, Texas Tech University, 1998.

Articles

Garland, Phyl. "The Lady Lives Jazz: Mary Lou Williams Remains as a Leading Interpreter of the Art." *Ebony* (October 1979): 56–64.

Williams, Mary Lou. "What I Learned from God about Jazz." *Sepia* (April 1958): 57–60.

Archival Sources

Eddie Bonnemère Papers. Schomburg Center for Research in Black Culture. New York Public Library.

Mary Lou Williams Collection. Institute of Jazz Studies. Rutgers University, Newark, NJ.

Melba Liston Archives. Center for Black Music Research. Columbia College Chicago.

Oral History of American Music (OHAM). Yale University, New Haven, CT.

Williams, Mary Lou. "Jazz Oral History Project." Interview by John S. Wilson. National Endowment for the Arts/Institute of Jazz Studies. Rutgers University, Newark, NJ.

Williams, Mary Lou. Letters to Dorothy Day. Dorothy Day-Catholic Worker Collection, Marquette University, Milwaukee, WI.

Films

Burke, Joanne. *Music on My Mind*. Produced by Joanne Burke and the Film and Video Workshop, 1988.

Index